LAWYER 2.0

How to Build a Six-Figure Solo Practice in 12 Months or Less: Essential Technology for Solo Practitioners

Joshua R. Williams, Esq.

ISBN: 978-0-615-45754-3

Cover image and design by Robert Pufahl

This book is dedicated to my family, especially my loving wife, Micki; my parents, Ted and Nancy; my mother-in-law, Ana; and my best men, Jeremy and Jesse. Thanks for the wisdom, the strength, and the love.

LAWYER 2.0 Contents

LAWYER 2.0 Introduction

I. GENESIS

After graduating from the University of Iowa College of Law in 2008, I accepted a job as an associate at one of the largest law firms in Minnesota. The rationale behind my decision to accept The Firm's offer was fairly simple: I liked the city, the people at The Firm seemed nice enough and were exceedingly competent, my job duties would involve using critical thinking skills, and, most importantly, the gig paid $120,000 per year. Like a walking cliché, I cast aside my dream of pursuing a career in public interest law—as memorialized in my sanctimonious law school application personal statement—the moment The Firm floated a few dollar signs in my direction.

For my first year at The Firm I was a glorified litigation paralegal and spent my time performing legal research on esoteric issues of law, drafting simple pleadings, reviewing documents, and carrying an occasional briefcase to court appearances. While the pay was good and my supervising attorney was great, I had some reservations about whether Biglaw was a good fit for me...

I did not like the fact that my duties did not involve direct interaction with clients.

I did not find arguing over patents and commercial contracts to be particularly meaningful work.

I did not like the fact that, for all intents and purposes, the unofficial expectation was that I was always "on call" if lawyers with more seniority than me needed me to perform a task they did not want to do themselves. In other words, The Firm owned me 24/7.

Finally, I absolutely loathed the hourly billing business model. Under the billable hour model, the lawyers law firms value the most are the lawyers who bill the most hours. Accordingly, the model creates perverse incentives for lawyers to be inefficient: to take longer to complete a project, bill more hours and thus become more valuable in the eyes of The Firm. This model directly contravened my work ethic given that I try to be as efficient as possible in everything I do.

Under The Firm's version of the billable hour model it required associates to bill 1,775 hours per year, which is slightly lower than the regional standard and much lower than yearly billable hours requirements at firms on the coasts or in Chicago. Even though associates "only" needed to bill 1,775 hours per year, that amount breaks down to about 7.3 hours per day. Note that we needed to ***bill*** 7.3 hours per day. So between lunch breaks, bathroom breaks, transitioning from project to project, etc., I found I needed to put in about nine to ten hours of office time in order to make my hours for the day. I tried to eat lunch at my desk as often as possible so I could leave the office at a reasonable hour, but I felt compelled to attend networking (internal and external) lunches and events two or three times per week, so I usually needed to stay at the office until 6:30 or 7:00 to make my hours.

Given that The Firm paid me $120,000 per year, working an 8:30 AM to 6:30 PM shift was not unreasonable. The problem, however, is that workflow tends to ebb and flow in litigation departments, even at big firms. Junior associates are entirely dependent on partners and senior associates for work assignments, and I had weeks where work was not trickling down to me and I had absolutely nothing to do. The Firm's expectation, however, was that I needed to be in the office during normal business hours in case work should materialize. When The Firm was busy, the unspoken expectation was that I should bill as many hours as possible (i.e., more than 16 hours a day if the work was there) to "make up" for slow months. This didn't seem fair to me because it wasn't like I was sipping mojitos in the Caribbean during slow months; I was still coming to work every day for 10 hours.

As much as I disliked working at The Firm, I just couldn't see myself walking away from a $120,000 salary given my six-figure student debt load.

Then I had what Will Meyerhofer refers to as an "Elevator Ride" moment.

Will Meyerhofer is a former Biglaw attorney who now works as a psychotherapist and writes a great blog called *The People's Therapist*, available at www.thepeoplestherapist.com. In a blog entry entitled "You Own This," he discusses the moment when he knew he wasn't cut out for Biglaw: when a senior attorney told him that he "owned" a big merger/acquisition deal during an elevator ride inside the client's corporate headquarters. Meyerhofer replied "Uh...really?" and, according to him, both he and the senior attorney knew at that moment he had "no intention of owning anything except [his] profound desire to get the hell out of [Biglaw]."

My Elevator Ride moment happened when I was light on work and asked one of the partners at The Firm if he needed help with anything. The partner, a great lawyer and an even better person, assigned me a legal research project involving one of his major clients. The client had purchased a $40 million yacht, yet the yacht suffered from several defects. The assignment was quite complex and involved international contract law because the seller of "the vessel" was located in the U.S., the seller's parent company was based in a European country, and delivery of "the vessel" took place in a different European country.

The client had a legitimate legal issue and needed help.

My problem was that I didn't really care about his legal issue and wasn't all that motivated to help him.

There aren't too many purchases more vulgar than a $40 million yacht, and I wanted to tell the client to go buy a kayak and donate $40 million to charity, or at least get a building at his alma mater's school of business named after him. When I got the yacht assignment, I realized I couldn't spend the rest of my legal career doing work I found so inconsequential and meaningless.

That was in Fall 2009, when legal jobs were scarcer than potatoes in Victorian-era Ireland. Unable to find a new job and unwilling to continue working at The Firm, I maxed out my credit cards, had second mortgages slapped on my house and vehicles, and basically put everything I had into starting my own civil rights firm.

In my first full year of solo practice, I earned more money—even after taxes and overhead—than I netted at The Firm. I was less than two years out of law school when I cleared my first $100,000 as a solo.

If I had known in Fall 2009 what I know now about law office technology I would have earned even more money. The reason why I decided to write this book was to help other solos avoid the frustrating and costly process of trial and error when implementing new technology into their practices. I cannot guarantee that the strategies I will share with you will get you to six figures; I am merely providing you with the tools to get there. If you incorporate my strategies and possess a modicum of competence, I predict you will be very satisfied with the results.

II. MY FIRM

I run a solo plaintiffs' litigation firm (www.jrwilliamslaw.com) in Minneapolis, Minnesota, representing clients in the areas of employment law, civil rights, and consumer protection.

I run a high-volume practice, and in order for me to earn six figures, I need to maintain between 30 and 40 active clients at all times. It is not easy *finding* 30 to 40 active clients because most potential clients who contact me do not have viable claims; in order for me to find one person I can help, I generally need to take at least 30 calls from potential new clients.

On a typical day I perform substantive work on five open files, speak with four existing clients on the phone, speak with two opposing counsel on the phone, file a new case in court, conduct eight initial phone consultations with potential clients, set two in-person client intake interviews, and conduct one in-person client intake interview.

I do not have any full-time staff: I have a law clerk who works remotely, a web developer I use on an a la carte basis, and a shared receptionist who greets my clients and lets me know when they arrive. Collectively, my "support staff" typically performs less than three hours of work per week for me.

Despite my heavy work load and lack of help, I rarely work more than 10 hours a day. More importantly, I have never missed a filing deadline, a court appearance, or even an appointment.

Ten years ago solos could not run a high-volume practice like mine without support; at the very least, they needed to hire a full-time legal secretary. With the technology that is available today, I can do it all on my own. In fact, one of the reasons why I have been so successful is *because* I do it all on my own: I know exactly what is going on in every single case at any given time, I can access my complete calendar at any time from my smartphone, I can access any file from any case at any time in seconds, and I am completely self-reliant.

I should note that I do not use technology just for the sake of using technology or to impress my friends and colleagues. Rather, I use technology for the sole purpose of running a more efficient practice. If certain technology does not save me time or make me money, then I do not incorporate it into my practice.

Finally, I must clarify that it is not like I just fell into a six-figure case during my first year of solo practice (and I certainly did not take any clients from The Firm when I left, with the exception of my pro bono clients). Rather, most of my cases are relatively small matters (i.e., generating fees of $15,000 or less), so it is fair to say that I genuinely built my practice up from nothing.

The keys to my high profits are organization, efficiency, and self-reliance, which combine to keep my overhead costs low. There are plenty of attorneys who collect more fees than I do but profit way less due to bloated overhead costs. If you incorporate the technology I use into your solo practice, I predict you will dramatically reduce your overhead without sacrificing the quality of your work product. Indeed, I predict the quality of your work product will *improve*.

III. HOW TO USE THIS BOOK

This book identifies and describes all the technology I used to build a six-figure solo practice in less than 12 months. I have decided to give away roughly half the contents of this book for free via posts on the *Lawyer 2.0* blog, available at www.lawyer2point0.com. To learn *all* the strategies I used to build a six-figure practice in less than 12 months you must purchase the book.

When I first started contemplating going solo I looked online and in bookstores for books on starting a law firm. The materials I located discussed issues such as psychological implications, ethical considerations, office location, where to meet clients, fee arrangements, what practice areas to specialize in, how to network, what furniture to purchase, and whether to offer clients coffee. All very important considerations. What I did not locate was a comprehensive "how-to" guide that summarized and described the technological tools solos need to get their practices up and running, find clients, and make money. This book fills that void.

Accordingly, this book is written for lawyers who have already started their own firm or made the decision to go solo. If you are still grappling with whether to hang a shingle, I recommend that you read the book *Solo by Choice* and the blog *MyShingle.com* (available at www.myshingle.com), both authored by Carolyn Elefant, which were instrumental in my own decision to go solo.

If you are ready to take the solo plunge and need practical information on how to efficiently run a firm and attract clients, or if you have been running a firm for several years and want to amplify your practice, this book is essential reading.

As set forth above, I could not locate any books aimed at solo practitioners that provided a comprehensive explanation of the technological tools solos need to launch (or amplify) their solo practices. That said, I located many publications, including books, magazines, and blogs, that discuss technology suitable for a law office. Many of the publications I located are aimed at a tech-savvy audience, and I had difficulty understanding the information contained therein. The publications I located aimed at lawyers contain plenty of useful information, but for various reasons they are not suitable for use as "how-to" guides to get a solo practice up and running from a technological standpoint. Thus, for the most part, I had to figure out on my own how to incorporate technology into my solo practice through trial and error. Some technology I identified enhanced my practice, some was unhelpful, and some just plain confusing (e.g., Google Wave).

The goal of this book is to take the guesswork out of what technology to incorporate into your solo practice. In that sense, this book is a "greatest hits" compilation album of technology I read about in various sources and tried out in my own practice.

This book is divided into six substantive chapters:

1. Hardware
2. Practice Management
3. The Paperless Law Office
4. Legal Research
5. Online Marketing
6. Other Considerations

Each chapter contains many subsections. I tried my best to craft each subsection so that you do not *need* to have read a previous section to get something out of a later section. That said, I encourage you to read the book in the order I wrote it, as I build on certain concepts throughout.

I wrote this book in plain English and used detailed illustrations to promote accessibility for lawyers who lack technological savvy. I have crafted this book in such a manner that you will find the materials contained herein useful even if you only possess a minimal understanding of how computers and office technology work.

I dubbed the PDF version of this publication a "webbook" because I intended readers to read it on a device with internet connectivity, as I included dozens of links to web pages you cannot access without an internet connection. Additionally, the webbook is password protected to prevent piracy, thus readers cannot print hard copies. For readers who desire hard copies, a paperback version of this book is available for purchase through the *Lawyer 2.0* companion website, available at www.lawyer2point0.com.

Finally, I should note that I limited the scope of this book to technology for solos because that is the only component of my practice I feel qualified to write a "how-to" book on at this early stage in my legal career. I recognize that there is a host of other factors that go into building a successful solo practice, and as a neophyte lawyer I concede I still have a lot to learn. The fact that I was able to build a six-figure practice in less than twelve months as a second-year attorney, however, underscores the profound positive impact effective use of technology can have on your solo practice.

LAWYER 2.0 Hardware

I. INTRODUCTION

This chapter identifies every piece of hardware I use in my solo practice (except for my phone system, which I will discuss in Chapter 2) and describes how I use it. The first substantive section discusses the "essential" hardware I use in my practice: hardware I absolutely could not do without. The second substantive section discusses the "bells and whistles" hardware I use in my practice: hardware I really like but could probably do without.

II. THE ESSENTIALS

A. Laptop or Desktop Computer

Your computer is the most important piece of hardware in your solo practice. As lawyers, we do not create products in the conventional sense because (in most cases) our core job function is to generate and manipulate documents. Thus, selecting the right computer is one of the most important decisions you make in your practice because your computer is the primary tool you will use to generate and manipulate documents.

When I launched my firm in Fall 2009, I grappled with whether to purchase a laptop or a desktop as my primary computer. I elected to purchase a laptop because I wanted the freedom to access my electronic files wherever I went, but I did not know how to use the Fujitsu ScanSnap scanner and Dropbox to run a paperless/digital law office at the time of purchase. The portability a laptop provides is less important now that my digital office enables me to access any document from every client file from any computer (or smartphone) with an internet connection. In fact, my laptop basically functions like a desktop, as I have rarely taken it outside my office since I implemented a mobile paperless/digital law office.

Laptops are generally slightly less powerful and more expensive than desktops, but at the end of the day the laptop/desktop choice is merely a matter of preference. I personally prefer laptops because they take up less space on your desk. Regardless of whether you decide to use a laptop or desktop, the most important consideration when purchasing a computer for your law office is speed; namely, processor speed, RAM, and hard drive RPM.

The processor (also referred to as the CPU, or central processing unit) is the brains of your computer and is the most important element of your computing system. The processor tells your computer what to do and when to do it, and decides which tasks are more important and prioritizes them to your computer's needs. Intel and AMD are the two primary makers of processors. Intel has greater name recognition, but the quality of AMD processors is comparable. Pretty much any processor that is pre-installed on a new computer is acceptable except for "budget processors" (i.e., Celeron and Duron), which are far too slow for an office setting.

RAM is an acronym for "random access memory" and provides space for your computer to read and write data to be accessed by the CPU. The more RAM your computer has, the fewer amount of times your CPU must read data from your hard disk. In other words, the more RAM your computer has, the faster it runs. Your office computer should have at least 4.00 GB of RAM.

Hard drive RPM, in short, refers to how fast your computer can access data on its hard drive. The slower the RPM, the longer it takes your computer to access your files. A computer equipped with a 7,200 RPM, 250 GB hard drive will provide solos with sufficient performance (and storage space).

The reason why you need a speedy computer is because you need your machine to multitask (i.e., run several programs simultaneously) throughout the day. If you purchase a computer equipped with a budget processor or a computer with a configuration aimed at home users or gamers, it will run your programs agonizingly slowly, costing you time and money.

As far as computer brands, if you have heard of the brand before (e.g., Sony, Dell, Toshiba, HP, etc.) you are in the clear; any manufacturer that survived the computer hardware wars is reputable, otherwise it would have gone out of business by now.

You can purchase a computer with an appropriate configuration for a law office for about $1,000.

Everything I know about appropriate computer configurations I learned from Barron Henley of Affinity Consulting Group (www.affinityconsulting.com) during a great CLE he frequently delivers at different locations across the country, "The $6,000 Law Office." I highly recommend you attend Mr. Henley's CLEs if he comes to your area.

The laptop I selected as my primary computer is the Toshiba Satellite L505:

Toshiba Satellite L505

Unfortunately, I purchased my Toshiba prior to attending Mr. Henley's CLE, and my machine only has a 5,400 RPM hard drive. Accordingly, it runs a little on the slow side. The computer came pre-loaded with the Vista Operating System, and I have not upgraded to Windows 7 because Mr. Henley cautioned against upgrading operating systems. According to him, your best option is to use the operating system pre-loaded on your computer. My Toshiba's battery life is lackluster, but because I use my laptop as a desktop replacement machine, battery life is a non-issue. Overall, I am satisfied, if not thrilled, with my Toshiba's performance.

A final issue is whether to purchase a PC or an Apple Macintosh. I do not see the Mac v. PC debate as an important issue for solos, as either system will do what you need it to do as long as it has adequate speed and memory. In short, I do not believe there is a right or wrong choice.

PC owners may argue that Macs are not real "business machines," but that statement has not been accurate since the Clinton Administration. In fact, every piece of hardware and software I use in my practice is Mac-compatible. Moreover, you can open and manipulate just about any file on a Mac that was originally generated on a PC and vice-versa.

Apple owners may argue that their machines are superior to PCs, but when pressed to explain why their Mac is so much better than my PC, the most articulate answer I ever get is "it just is." It may be the case that Macs possess superior audio and video editing capabilities, but we are lawyers, not auteur music video directors, thus editing capability is not an important consideration when deciding on a computer.

I believe Macs and PCs are both appropriate in a business setting. I purchased a PC because I have used PCs exclusively since I was in high school and therefore felt comfortable with the Windows interface. Thus, if you have been using a PC up to this point, there is no need to switch to a Mac. Conversely, if you feel comfortable with Macs, there is no good reason to switch to a PC besides the fact that PCs are considerably less expensive.

B. Netbook

As set forth in the preceding subsection, your primary computer must have sufficient speed and memory. With the exception of the MacBook Air, any laptop that possesses the requisite speed and memory is going to be somewhat bulky (my Toshiba weighs about six pounds). I travel fairly often and my practice requires me to make frequent court appearances, and I wanted a computer that wasn't such a hassle to lug around. I contemplated purchasing a netbook—a small, lightweight laptop computer—to replace my Toshiba, but netbooks' speed and memory are inferior to laptops and I did not want to sacrifice performance for portability. Another reason why traveling with my computer was challenging for me was because I would get paranoid about losing all my files should something happen to my laptop.

Implementing a paperless/digital law office proved to be the remedy to my portability problem. By implementing a mobile paperless/digital law office that enables me to access any document from every client file from any computer with an internet connection, I can use my Toshiba as my primary document generating machine and use a netbook to access documents when I am on the go. In most cases I do not even need an active internet connection to access documents from my netbook because Dropbox (which I discuss in greater detail in Chapter 3) automatically syncs documents on machines linked to the same Dropbox account.

I also like having a netbook because it serves as my home computer and as a backup computer should my Toshiba crash. I do not get paranoid about losing my files should something happen to my netbook because all my files are saved in several different locations, including my Toshiba's hard drive, an external hard drive, and "the Cloud" (i.e., online).

You should not utilize a netbook as your main computer. Rather, a netbook is a great on-the-go/complementary computer that you should use primarily for data consumption as opposed to data generation. Accordingly, your netbook does not need as much muscle under its hood as your primary computer. Your netbook should, however, have at least 1 GB of RAM and an Intel Atom processor or equivalent.

The netbook I purchased is an HP Mini 210-1180 NR:

HP Mini 210-1180 NR

My HP weighs about three pounds, is super-compact, and came pre-loaded with the Windows 7 Starter operating system. I purchased my HP for only $250 (at Office Max), so I do not freak out if it gets a little wear and tear in transit. The monitor is smallish but serviceable, and while the keyboard is not quite full-size, it's close enough that it doesn't bother me (and at 6'5 I have fairly large hands). Additionally, its battery life is excellent. In short, the machine does everything I need it to do and I highly recommend it.

C. **Fujitsu ScanSnap s1500**

You need to buy the ScanSnap s1500:

Fujitsu ScanSnap s1500

An all-in-one printer with a built-in scanner is not going to cut it for your scanning needs. I implore you to purchase a ScanSnap s1500 for each member of your team who routinely handles and files hard copies of documents.

Richard Keyt, one of the pioneers of the paperless/digital law office, explains why you need to bite the bullet and pony up for a quality, dedicated personal scanner like the ScanSnap on his website, available at www.keytlaw.com:

The scanners you see in computer stores like Best Buy, CompUSA and Circuit City are slow home-use scanners. When you shop for an office scanner, you want speed (at least 20 pages per minute) and a sheet feeder that takes at least 25 pages. If the scanner on sale doesn't prominently display its pages per minute scanning speed, it means the scanner is much too slow (a few pages per minute) to use for anything other than infrequent home scanning. I bought three HP 3380 4 in 1 printer, scanner, fax and copiers for $700. They print, fax and copy great, but the fastest I could ever get the HP 3380 to scan was 2 pages per minute in black and white at 300 dpi. Very fast high volume scanners are several thousand dollars and up, but most small offices don't need that kind of speed (50+ pages per minute). Manufacturers of medium and high speed scanners display the scanner speed because that is one of the main features buyers seek.

I purchased my ScanSnap on www.newegg.com for about $400. I will explain in Chapter 3 how the ScanSnap is the backbone of a paperless/digital office.

D. <u>All-in-One Printer</u>

I have referred to running a paperless office on several occasions in this chapter, but the term "paperless," is a bit of a misnomer. While I convert hard copies of every document I receive into digital files, I still need to print hard copies of documents regularly in my practice; unfortunately, not everyone in my professional orbit, including clients, some courts, and opposing counsel, has joined the digital revolution.

Until recently the conventional wisdom was that only laser printers could fulfill even a small office's printing needs, and that inkjet printers were only appropriate for home use (i.e., for printing photos from cheap digital cameras and printing occasional documents). This is because lasers far outperformed inkjets in terms of printing costs, print speed, and text detail. The primary drawbacks to lasers are that they are generally more expensive than inkjets and the quality of color images printed on lasers is lackluster.

It is crucially important that my printer possess color printing capabilities because I print documents on my firm letterhead directly from Word files, and my letterhead contains color images. To clarify, I do not manually feed pre-printed firm letterhead every time I want to print a document on firm letterhead; I just open up a template in Word, type, and print.

What I need in a printer is a machine that combines the strengths of lasers and inkjets. Specifically, I need a machine that prints high-quality color documents quickly and cheaply at a reasonable price.

The solution: The HP Officejet Pro 8500:

HP Officejet Pro 8500 All-in-One Printer

The Officejet is one of a handful of inkjet all-in-one printers aimed at small offices, and it prints laser-quality documents at laser-quality speeds. Most importantly, the Officejet prints documents even more cheaply than lasers due to its high-capacity ink cartridges. Finally, the quality of color images printed on the Officejet is beautiful.

The Officejet would be worth its $250 price tag based on its printing capabilities alone, but it also serves as a fax machine, a scanner, and a copier. I do not use the Officejet scanner function frequently because the ScanSnap meets most of my scanning needs, but every now and then I need to scan in a document that does not work well with the ScanSnap's automatic document feeder (e.g., a torn receipt). I will place such documents on the Officejet's flatbed and scan them right onto my computer's hard drive. Even though I use the Officejet's scanner function infrequently, I would nonetheless purchase a separate flatbed scanner if the Officejet did not come equipped with one because maintaining a paperless/digital office requires me to religiously scan hard copies of *every* document I receive.

I use the Officejet copier function about once every two weeks. I typically use the ScanSnap's scan-to-print function that enables users to feed up to 50 pages in its automatic document feeder and print directly to their printers when I need to make copies. Many of my clients, however, need copies of frayed documents that the ScanSnap's automatic document feeder does not handle particularly well, and I use the Officejet's flatbed to capture the image. Thus, I would purchase a separate copier if the Officejet did not come equipped with a copier function.

Finally, I do not use the Officejet fax function at all because I use an internet fax service that enables users to send and receive faxes via e-mail. I will, of course, discuss this service in greater detail in later sections of this book.

E. Dymo Labelwriter 450 Twin Turbo and Digital Postage Scale

I send documents via e-mail as attachments whenever possible because doing so saves time and money. That said, I send documents via snail mail fairly frequently, as some of my clients do not have reliable internet access and a substantial minority of lawyers and courts still prefer receiving hard copies of documents. As a plaintiffs' lawyer I also frequently send out pre-suit demand packages to putative defendants, and I deliver them via e-mail, fax, and snail mail (the snail mail version can weigh up to 16 ounces).

I typically sue Fortune 1000 companies and go up against some of the largest law firms in the Midwest, and if the other side does not view me as a formidable adversary such underestimation can—and will—adversely affect my ability to achieve favorable outcomes for my clients. Accordingly, any materials that leave my office ***must*** look professional.

Hand writing the recipient's address and my return address on an envelope does not look professional, especially given that my handwriting looks like a second grader's.

Using several stamps on an envelope does not look professional either.

Avery sheet mailing labels are ideal for printing return address labels because you can print a few sheets at one time and use individual labels on an as-needed basis. Printing the recipient's address is a different story, as you need to manually feed the label sheet into your printer every time you need to print an address label and utilize Microsoft Word to tell the printer the precise row and column of the single label you want the printer to print on (for whatever reason, I muff this transaction roughly 45 percent of the time).

My postage system was even less efficient than my labeling system. For mailings that fit in a regular envelope I just used a forever stamp and called it a day, which is acceptable. As I mentioned earlier, I send out mailings that weigh more than one ounce fairly regularly, and using several stamps on one envelope looks unprofessional. Additionally, over-stamping cost me at least a few dollars each month.

I did not mail enough documents to justify renting a postage meter for $20 per month, the USPS's online pay and click service (available at http://tinyurl.com/camax) is grossly overpriced, and dealing with lines at the post office every time I wanted to send a letter that weighed more than one ounce was not a viable option.

For the reasons set forth above, the gaping hole in my solo practice efficiency game was labeling and postage, as preparing a piece of mail that weighed more than one ounce was a 10 to 15 minute operation. In a high-volume practice with no full-time staff, I do not have 15 minutes to spare for one piece of mail.

The solution: The Dymo Labelwriter 450 Twin Turbo:

Dymo Labelwriter 450 Twin Turbo

The Labelwriter 450 is a thermal label printer, which means I do not ever need to worry about replacing ink cartridges. The Labelwriter 450 connects directly to my laptop via USB cable and features two spools, one for labels and one for stamps.

For labeling, the Labelwriter 450 enables me to create labels directly from text in Microsoft Word without retyping. Alternatively, I can open the software that comes with the Labelwriter 450 and type and print an address label in seconds.

For postage, all I need to do is load an account on Endicia (www.endicia.com) with credit and print stamps on an a la carte basis (for standard letters I just use one forever stamp). I can easily print exact postage by weighing my mailings with a digital postage scale; if I know the weight, the software that comes with the Labelwriter 450 tells me the exact amount of postage I need.

I purchased the Labelwriter 450 for about $200 from Office Max and my digital scale from the post office about $30. The hardware will probably pay for itself in over-stamping savings alone. The time and hassle the Labelwriter 450 save me are priceless.

F. Seagate Replica

The Seagate Replica is the ultimate backup solution for solos.

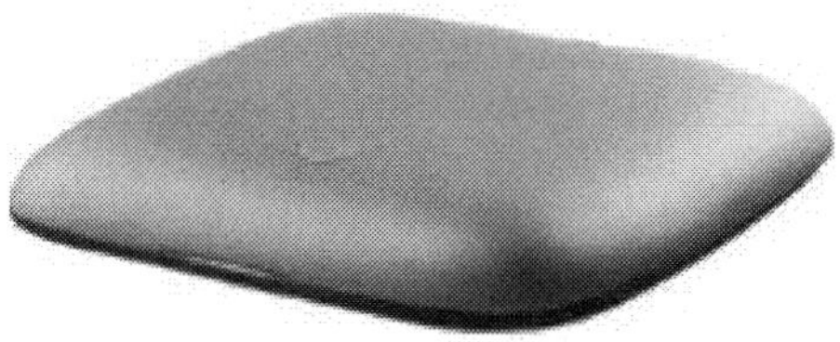

Seagate Replica

I need a backup solution that backs up my computer's entire hard drive (including programs and operating system, not just data files like Word documents, music, photos, video, etc.), and does so automatically. That is, anytime I modify something on my hard drive, including adding a new program, deleting a program, or modifying a file, I need a device or program that automatically captures the modification without me having to do so manually. The Seagate Replica does exactly that.

The Replica is a small (0.7 by 5.7 by 4 inches, HWD) external hard drive that connects to your computer via a USB cable. Once you connect the device to your computer all you need to do is press ok on a dialog box a few times and it automatically starts backing up your entire hard drive. If you keep the Replica plugged in, it will continuously back up any changes to your computer's hard drive. If you add or modify your hard drive when the Replica is not connected to your computer, the device will capture the modification when you reconnect. If you accidentally delete a file or folder, you can retrieve it from the Replica in seconds.

The Replica comes with a recovery disc that lets you boot up a crashed computer and restore your hard drive in about an hour. If your computer is stolen or damaged beyond repair, you can recover all your files and folders from your Replica and transfer them onto your replacement computer in minutes. The Replica comes in 250 GB and 500 GB versions. I purchased the 500 GB version for about $130 on www.newegg.com.

In later sections I will discuss two additional data backup systems I use in my practice.

G. Targus Chill Hub XC for Laptops

I use four peripheral devices that connect to my Toshiba laptop via USB connection, but my laptop has only three USB ports. The solution: The Targus Chill Hub XC for Laptops:

Targus Chill Hub XC for Laptops

The Chill Hub also connects to my Toshiba via a USB connection, but features four USB ports for peripheral devices. Thus, I keep my printer, ScanSnap, Replica, and Labelwriter connected to the Chill Hub, and my Toshiba automatically connects to those devices when I connect my laptop to the Chill Hub: a simple, easy, and convenient solution for connecting my computer to my peripheral devices each day.

As its name implies, the Chill Hub also provides cooling for my Toshiba via dual USB-powered fans and acts as a heat barrier between my laptop and desk. A quick perusal of online customer reviews shows that some users are less than thrilled with the Chill Hub's performance, but after over one year of use it has not given me any problems. I purchased the Chill Hub for about $40 at Office Max.

I should also note that there are more elaborate docking stations available for connecting peripheral devices to your laptop, but I like the Chill Hub because of the built-in cooling fans.

H. <u>Wireless Router</u>

I use a laptop rather than a desktop computer, and I store my machine in a file cabinet before I leave the office each day. I connected my landlord-issued DSL line to a wireless router because I did not want the hassle of plugging the line into my computer every day. Even if I used a desktop, I would still use a wireless router because I have a law clerk who occasionally works at the desk that sits outside my office (he does most of his work remotely), and he can get an internet connection through my wireless network.

I purchased the Linksys WRT54G2 Wireless-G Router

Linksys Wireless-G Router

from Office Max for about $45 and have no complaints.

I. Notary Stamp

The final piece of essential hardware I will discuss, my notary stamp,

Notary Stamp

is conspicuously old school. Nonetheless, it plays a very important role in my practice. As a litigator I frequently need my clients to sign documents that require notarization (e.g., interrogatories, affidavits, etc.), and as a plaintiffs' litigator who represents actual people my clients typically are not "sophisticated" clients with assistants who are licensed notaries.

Many of my clients do not drive, so having a document notarized can be a big hassle for them. They appreciate the fact that they can come to my office and I can notarize the document myself, or I will come to them, if necessary.

My notary registration fees were about $150 (annual renewal fees are about $40) and I purchased my self-inking stamp from Office Max for about $30.

III. BELLS & WHISTLES

A. Microsoft LifeCam and MXL AC404 Microphone

As a litigator I take depositions fairly often in my practice. I like video recording my depositions because I find that both the deponent and opposing counsel tend to stay in line when they know the camera is watching. If they get out of line, then I can show their video-recorded misconduct to a judge or jury. Most of my cases are relatively small matters (i.e., under $50,000), and the four-figure professional videographer fee is cost prohibitive. A serviceable solution has been to use the Windows LifeCam and MXL AC404 microphone to video record depositions on my own:

Microsoft LifeCam   MXL AC404 Microphone

Both devices are about the size of a computer mouse and connect to my netbook via extra-long USB cables. I point the LifeCam at the deponent, place the high-powered MXL microphone just about anywhere in the room, and simply press a button on the software that comes with the LifeCam to start recording. The video file saves straight to my computer's hard drive, and I can easily transfer the file to a recordable DVD. The final product is not something I would enter in the Cannes Film Festival, as it looks somewhat pixilated and vaguely amateurish, but the audio and video sync up and you can hear voices clearly. Accordingly, I would not hesitate to show it to a judge or jury.

I purchased the LifeCam for about $100 on Amazon and the MXL for about $75 on Amazon. For a big case I would probably bite the bullet and pay for a professional videographer, but for my smaller cases the LifeCam/MXL combo is an economical method of taking do-it-yourself video depositions.

B. Portable DVD Player

I had a client perform so poorly at a deposition that her testimony nearly cost us the case. I spent a considerable amount of time preparing her for her deposition, but once the defendant's lawyer started asking questions she abandoned our strategy faster than Rocky ditched Apollo's game plan for Balboa-Lang II. As I watched the defense lawyer repeatedly land metaphorical combinations and uppercuts on my client, it became apparent that she could have benefited from having seen an actual deposition so she would have had a better idea of what to expect.

Peter Barry of Barry & Slade, LLC (www.lawpoint.com), who is the preeminent Fair Debt Collection Practices Act lawyer in the country (and who travels across the country putting on Boot Camps (www.fdcpabootcamp.com) teaching lawyers how to litigate FDCPA cases), has solved the deposition disaster problem by requiring his clients to view a deposition preparation DVD produced by the

Wisconsin Bar Association. The aptly named DVD, *Preparing for Your Deposition*, features accurate dramatizations that show what a deposition is like. I purchased a copy of the DVD from Amazon for about $130. Now, I prepare my clients for their depositions by setting them up in a conference room with a portable DVD player I purchased from Target for under $50 and instructing them to watch the DVD and review documents from their cases.

A deposition can make or break a case, and the cost of the DVD and DVD player will pay for itself in spades in one case if your client gives a solid deposition that s/he may have otherwise botched.

C. Tablet Computer

A tablet computer is a portable personal computer equipped with a touchscreen as a primary input device. The Apple iPad is the current tablet market leader.

I do not own a tablet computer because I thought its features were redundant vis-à-vis my netbook. In fact, I determined that my netbook was superior to a tablet because it enables me to manipulate and generate data rather than merely consume it. Murad Mohammad's description of how he uses his iPad in his criminal defense practice on his blog, *Maclawgic* (available at www.maclawg.wordpress.com), forced me to reevaluate my position.

Mr. Mohammad uses his iPad for several purposes, including as his trial notebook. Specifically, he loads all his trial documents and notes, including police reports, medical reports (all saved as digital files), and even audio and video files onto his iPad. During trial, it only takes him a few seconds to access a document. Thus, when Murad shows up for trial he does not lug around multiple dog-eared accordion files and yellowed banker's boxes, as everything he needs is stored neatly onto his iPad. Unlike a netbook, the iPad fits right into the palm of his hand and he can use it when he is on his feet examining a witness or addressing the judge or the jury.

I do not go to trial very often, but I engage in enough oral advocacy that adding the freedom and flexibility of a tablet to my courtroom practice makes sense. I have not purchased an iPad or any of the alternatives that run on the Android operating system yet because I am waiting for the Google tablet, the G-Slate, to come out. As you will learn in later sections of this book, I am somewhat of a Googlephile, thus I feel compelled to see what Google brings to the table before I invest in a tablet. If the G-Slate is not up to par, then I will probably purchase an iPad because the Android alternatives have received mixed reviews.

D. <u>Wireless Mouse</u>

On most days I do not mind using my laptop's touchpad, but every so often my hands cramp up. On those days I use a Belkin wireless mouse:

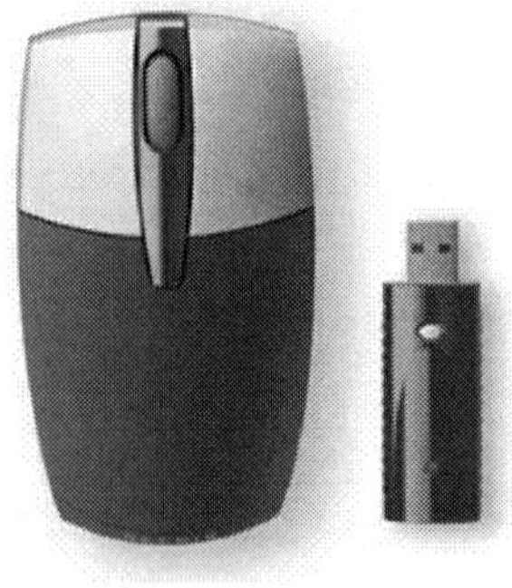

Belkin Wireless Mouse

I purchased the mouse from Office Max for under $15. I chose a wireless model because space is at a premium on my desk and I did not want to deal with additional wires. To activate the mouse you simply insert batteries in the device and the wireless receiver into a USB port on your computer.

LAWYER 2.0 Practice Management

I. INTRODUCTION

The title of this chapter, "Practice Management," is somewhat of a misnomer, as every tool I use in my law firm involves practice management in some way, shape, or form. For organization and clarity, I have restricted the scope of this chapter to a discussion of technology I use to facilitate communication and to keep track of my cases.

II. E-MAIL: GMAIL FOR BUSINESS

E-mail is the most important tool modern lawyers use to communicate. Some old-school lawyers take the position that e-mail is too informal and argue that lawyers should generally stick to traditional means of communicating such as phone calls and letters, and only use e-mail in rare circumstances. These same lawyers also believe dictating documents is an efficient use of a lawyer's time (it's not).

In contrast, some so-called "social media experts" argue that e-mail is *too* formal and take the position that "the future" lies in texting and Facebook IM. These are also the same people who believe it is appropriate to text during meetings (it's not).

The fact is that e-mail is generally always appropriate in a business setting and a "future" where text messages and IMs are has yet to arrive. The only situations when e-mail is never appropriate are where (1) a client does not have reliable internet access, (2) your judge does not feel comfortable using e-mail, (3) e-mail communications with opposing counsel have reached a stalemate, or (4) you need to break some heavy news and a phone or face-to-face conversation is more appropriate. Other than those four situations, I use e-mail almost exclusively to communicate with existing clients and lawyers.

Disclaimer: I concede that certain situations merit a more formal communication (e.g., settlement letters, disengagement letters, etc.) on firm letterhead, but in such situations I generally draft a letter on Word, save it as a PDF file, and attach the document to an e-mail.

As for texts and IMs, the only situation where I text or IM in my practice is when a client lacks reliable internet access, but I will only text or IM if all other means of attempted communication have proven to be futile.

E-mail is simple, efficient, and versatile. It obviates the need for phone tag, which can take hours away from other important tasks. It eliminates the lag time of snail mail, which can slow a case down for days or weeks. It saves me (and my clients) hundreds (if not thousands) of dollars in yearly postage and printing costs. Possibly most importantly, I can send an e-mail from anywhere at any time from any device with an internet connection, including my smartphone.

Used properly, e-mail is the most important arrow in a solo's technological quiver except for your computer.

All solos should use Gmail for Business as their e-mail client. I used Outlook for many years in a variety of office settings, so I am sympathetic to Outlook users (Outlookers?) who are resistant to change. That said, Gmail for Business is the best e-mail option for solos because it is cheaper, easier to use, more secure, and generally superior to Outlook.

Gmail is e-mail in the Cloud, which means Google stores your e-mail online and you can access your account from any device with an internet connection, including your smartphone. Gmail has virtually unlimited storage, which means you never need to worry about deleting an e-mail or taking up space on your hard drive. If you insist on having desktop access to your e-mail account to protect against your internet connection going down, then you can enable the Gmail "offline" feature which automatically stores duplicates of all your e-mails (and your calendar) on your hard drive.

You must subscribe to Google Apps for Business (visit http://tinyurl.com/y9ygvdt) for $50 each year per user to use Gmail for Business. Visit http://tinyurl.com/2vppzw5 to migrate e-mail, calendar, and contacts from Outlook to Gmail for Business.

Finally, Gmail for Business is secure. I suppose a highly motivated hacker could hack into Google's remote servers, but I imagine a semi-motivated common thief could break into your office and steal your firm's server. In other words, you are not sacrificing security by abandoning Microsoft Outlook to use Gmail for Business.

The following subsections highlight several features within Gmail for Business I frequently use in my practice.

A. Brand Your E-mail Address

Using an "@gmail.com" e-mail address is not an option for solos. It looks unprofessional and signals to colleagues, clients, courts, and opposing counsel that your firm is a small-time operation without any infrastructure. Fortunately, Gmail for Business enables you to import e-mail addresses with your branded domain name into your Gmail account by taking the following steps (if you already own a branded e-mail address skip to Step 3):

1. Go to your domain registrar control panel and create an e-mail forwarding account for your domain (most registrars (e.g., GoDaddy) offer this feature for free with your domain registration).
2. Decide what your branded e-mail address will be (for example, JWILLIAMS@JRWILLIAMSLAW.COM) and forward it to your Gmail address. You do this by filling up two fields in your domain registrar's e-mail forwarding control panel:

- In the “Add Forward” field, type in the left portion of your branded e-mail address, in this example JWILLIAMS.
- In the “Forward Mail To” field, type in your current Gmail address.

3. Log on to **Gmail.**
4. Click on **Settings** (you’ll find the link in the top right corner).
5. Click on **Accounts.**
6. Click on **Add Another Email Address.**
7. Add your new, branded address: JWILLIAMS@JRWILLIAMSLAW.COM
8. Click on the **Next Steps** button.
9. Click on the **Send Verification** button. Gmail will now send you a message with a link that you must click to verify that in fact you own your branded domain. Since in Step 2 you have already forwarded your branded address to your Gmail address, the verification e-mail will be automatically forwarded to your regular Gmail address.
10. Open the verification e-mail and click on the verification link.
11. Go back to the **Accounts** tab of the **Settings** menu.
12. Click on the link that says ‘**make default**’ next to your branded address.
13. Check the radio button next to “**always reply from my default address**.”

And you’re done.

Gmail for Business will now import any e-mails sent to your branded e-mail address, and any e-mails going out of your Gmail for Business account will show as coming from your branded e-mail address:

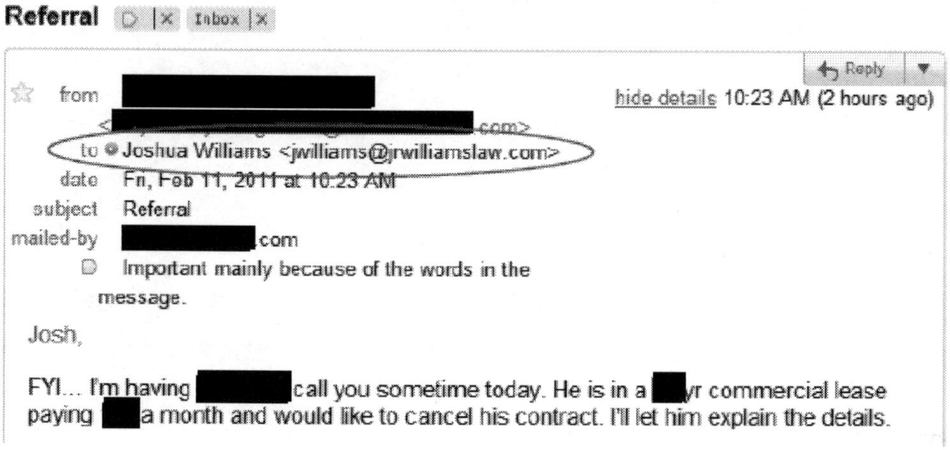
Referral Inbox

Reply

from [redacted]

<[redacted].com>

to Joshua Williams <jwilliams@jrwilliamslaw.com>

hide details 10:23 AM (2 hours ago)

date Fri, Feb 11, 2011 at 10:23 AM

subject Referral

mailed-by [redacted].com

Important mainly because of the words in the message.

Josh,

FYI... I'm having [redacted] call you sometime today. He is in a [redacted]yr commercial lease paying [redacted] a month and would like to cancel his contract. I'll let him explain the details.

Note: If you experienced any difficulty implementing the steps above, visit Gmail's custom domain help page, available at http://tinyurl.com/yv2xaf.

B. Labels

Gmail does not use the familiar folder system that Outlook uses to categorize e-mail messages, and instead uses what it calls Labels. Visit Gmail's Labels help page at http://tinyurl.com/cddx6e to learn how to use Labels. Jim Barr explains how labels work on his blog, *Gmail Tips* (available at http://tinyurl.com/4sdl6wc):

> Gmail lets you assign a Label to a message and then view all messages assigned to that Label. Sounds a lot like the typical "Folder," right? Well, almost. Unlike Folders, you can assign multiple Labels to a message letting the message span multiple categories. To better understand how Labels differ from Folders, consider the real-world counterparts, and it should become clear.

Say you have a desk full of paper messages, some messages are from family members, and some are jokes that your friends have sent you. Using the Folder model to categorize the messages, you would create one folder called "Family" and one called "Jokes." You would then look through the paper messages and file them accordingly. Simple and effortless. When you want to look for a message from your father, you just look in the "Family" folder. But wait. One of the messages is from your Mother, AND it is a joke. Which folder do you file it in? That's the dilemma with Folders.

OK, back to the desk full of paper messages. Now, instead of having folders, say you have sheets of labels, some marked "Family" and some marked "Jokes." You affix "Family" labels to all messages from your family, and you affix "Jokes" labels to all messages that are jokes. Your Mother's message simply now has two labels on it. When you want to see all Family messages, you just grab all the messages that have "Family" labels. Some may also have "Jokes" labels, but you don't care because you are interested in your Family messages. Likewise, when you grab all the messages labeled "Jokes," some may also have "Family" labels, but again, you don't care because you are looking at Jokes. Further, if you only want to look at jokes from your family, you grab only the messages with BOTH "Family" AND "Jokes" labels.

Here is a screen shot that captures Jim Barr's example:

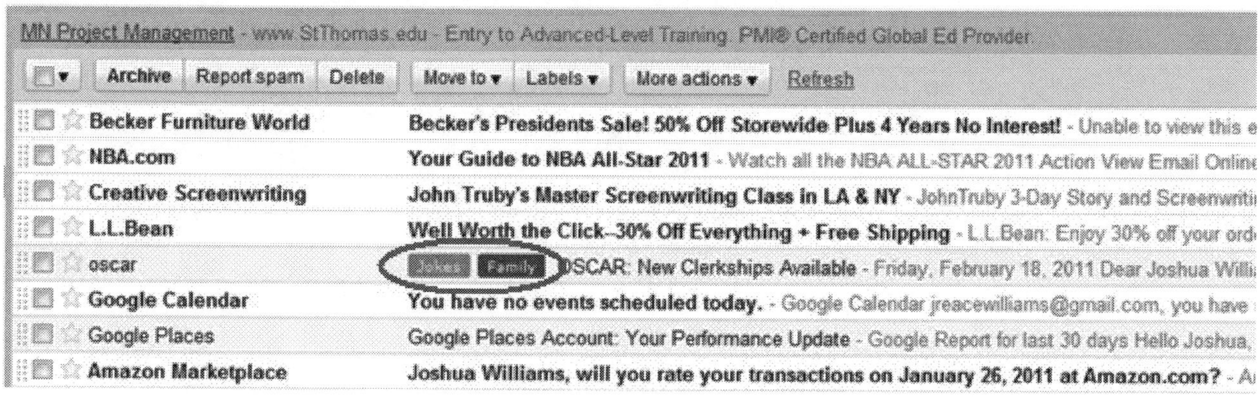

Families and jokes aside, I did not particularly care for Labels when I first started using Gmail for Business. Like communism and the deep fried bacon cheeseburger, Labels seemed great in theory but did not work particularly well in practice. My primary issue was that I quickly got to the point where I had too many labels, as I assign a label to each client:

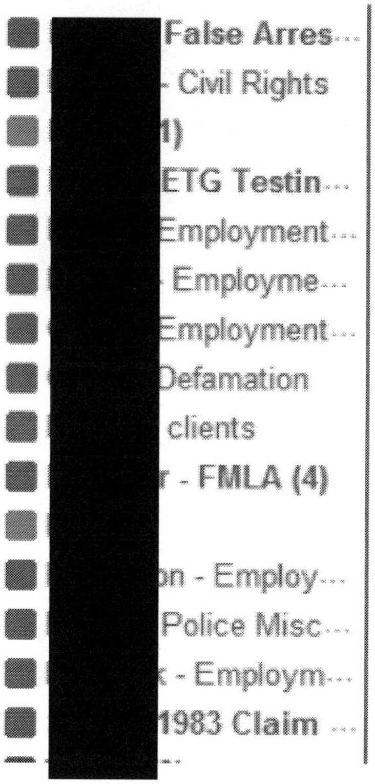

I operate a high-volume practice, thus my label system quickly became unwieldy (removing a label once a current client turned into a former client was not an option because I frequently need to refer back to e-mails from closed cases and I wanted to retain the label identifier). A secondary problem was that I missed the familiar drag and drop feature from Outlook. As set forth below, Google has implemented fixes for my issues and now I am a huge fan of Labels.

C. <u>Nested Labels</u>

Nested Labels enable users to "nest" sub-labels under parent labels, and to expand and collapse the parent label:

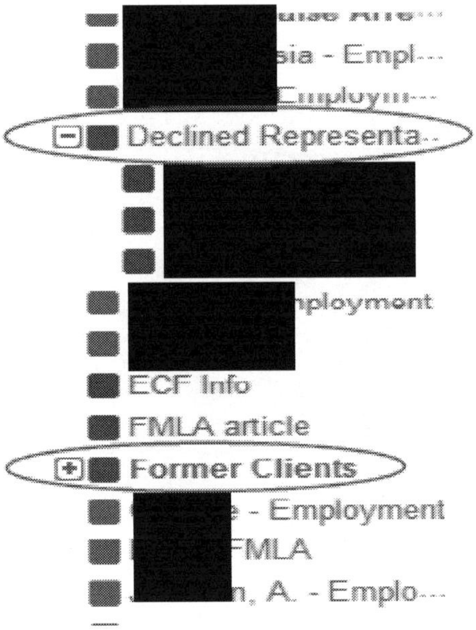

Now I just nest former client labels under a "Former Clients" parent label, and expand the parent label when necessary:

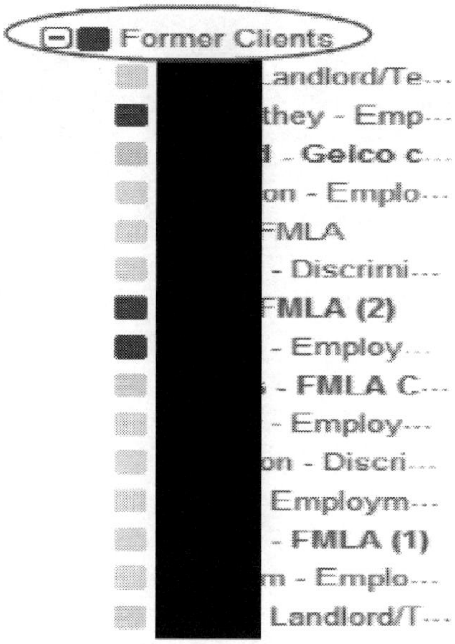

My labels system is now manageable.

To enable Nested Labels click on **Settings** in your Gmail account, click on **Labs**, scroll down until you see "Nested Labels" and press the corresponding **Enable** radio button.

D. <u>Drag and Drop</u>

Google didn't *need* to tweak Gmail to enable users to drag and drop messages into labels, just like you can with Outlook folders:

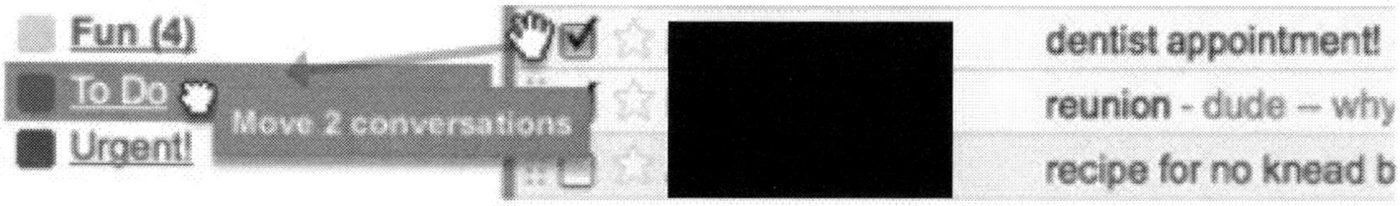

It is a cute feature, but the way Labels work it's vaguely superfluous. Kinda like the parsley that sits on top of a steak dinner.

The feature that truly enhances the Gmail experience is enabling users to drag and drop labels onto messages:

I have found that this feature saves me a ton of time, as I can move multiple messages at once by selecting the messages and then dragging and dropping the label.

E. <u>Canned Responses</u>

Unfortunately, I cannot help the majority of potential clients who contact me because they do not have viable claims. Potential new clients often send me long e-mails describing their legal issues, and I found myself composing the same types of responses over and over (even if I do not feel a potential client has a viable claim or I otherwise do not want to work with him/her, I *always* respond if someone reaches out to me because it is the right thing to do). Enabling Canned Responses obviates the need to compose the same reply to common questions.

With Canned Responses you can compose a reply once and save the message text with the "Canned Response" button. You will assign your canned response a name, and when you want to reply with a canned response just select the appropriate canned response:

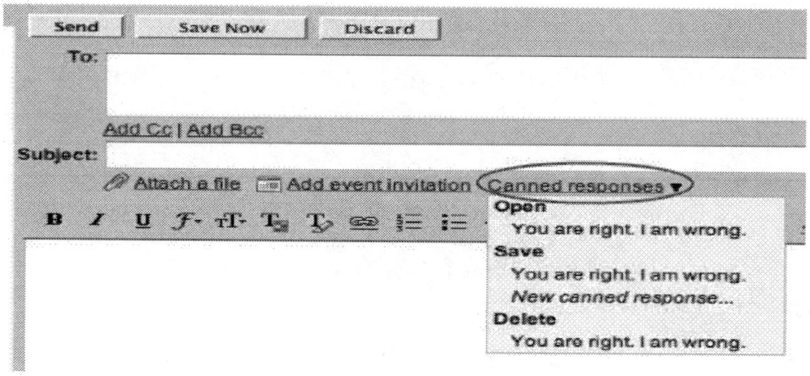

This feature probably saves me at least two hours of time per month. To enable Canned Responses click on **Settings** in your Gmail account, click on **Labs**, scroll down until you see "Canned Responses" and press the corresponding **Enable** radio button.

F. Signature Tweaks

Gmail defaults to positioning your signature block at the very bottom of a reply e-mail. This bothered me because when potential clients sent me inquiry e-mails, the signature block in my response was positioned below their original message. I felt this looked unprofessional, so my unwieldy fix was to copy and paste my signature block directly below the body of my response. Signature Tweaks fixes my issue by positioning my signature block before the quoted text in a response.

To enable Signature Tweaks click on **Settings** in your Gmail account, click on **Labs**, scroll down until you see "Signature Tweaks" and press the corresponding **Enable** radio button.

G. Desktop Notifications

Another feature I missed from Outlook was the floating notifications that popped up on my desktop when I received a new e-mail, but Google, once again, remedied my issue.

To enable new mail notifications, click on **Settings**, click on **General**, scroll down until you see "Desktop Notifications," and click on the "New mail notifications on" radio button:

H. Undo Send

All e-mail users have sent an e-mail and instantly regretted hitting the send button. Such gaffes can cause you embarrassment in a social setting, and in an office setting they can cost you money.

Gmail's undo send feature provides users with a 30-second window to undo a sent e-mail. If you want to undo a sent e-mail, simply hit the "Undo" button:

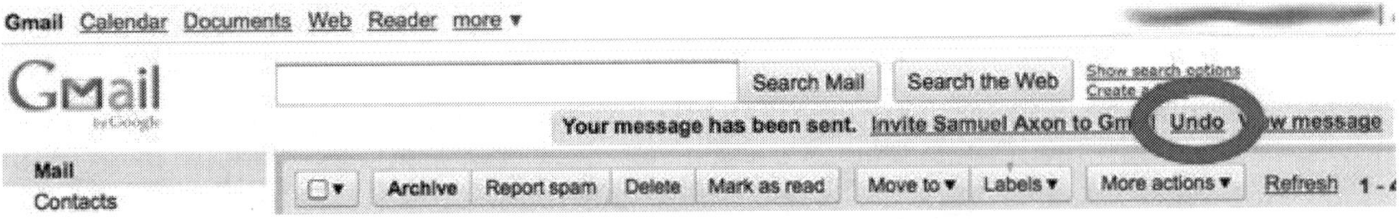

Gmail will then direct you back to the composition page:

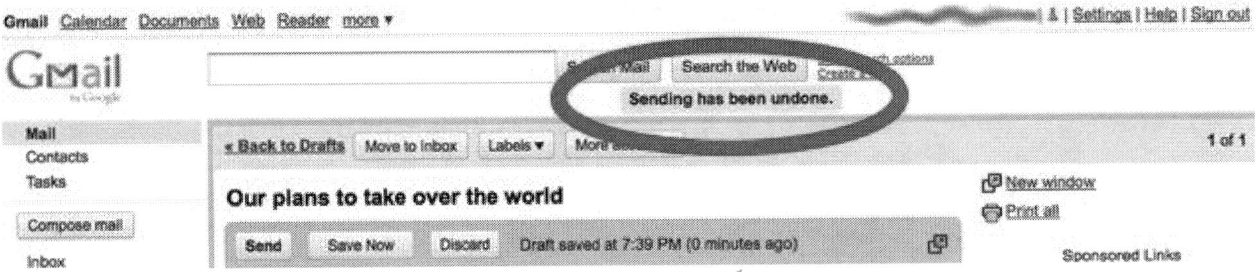

To enable Undo Send click on **Settings** in your Gmail account, click on **Labs**, scroll down until you see "Undo Send" and press the corresponding **Enable** radio button.

I. Pointofmail.com

One of Gmail's drawbacks used to be that users could not track whether intended e-mail recipients received their transmissions. Thus, if I sent a client an e-mail and did not receive a response I did not know whether she was willfully ignoring my communication or if I merely sent the e-mail to the wrong address.

Pointofmail.com alleviates the insecurity I experienced with Gmail by notifying me when my sent e-mails are read, where they are opened, and for how long they are viewed, among other things:

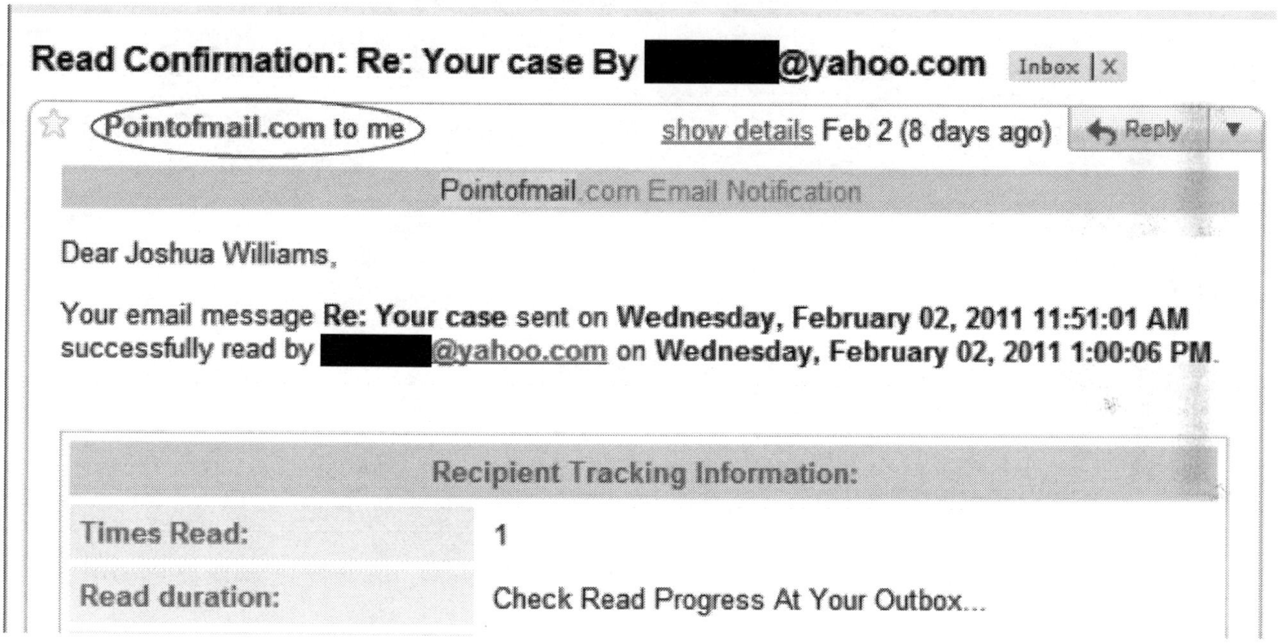

After you create an account at www.pointofmail.com, all you need to do is add "pointofmail.com" at the end of recipients' e-mail addresses (the "pointofmail.com" suffix is invisible to recipients) and Pointofmail.com will send you time-stamped e-mail confirmations when recipients read your e-mail or open attachments.

Pointofmail.com service costs $29.99 for one year with 2,500 e-mails.

J. GmailDefaultMaker

Another problem with Gmail used to be that when you clicked on a "mailto" link on a web page, Windows would try to open Outlook, Windows Live Mail, or some other program you don't use and have not configured (i.e., not your Gmail account).

You can fix this problem by installing GmailDefaultMaker, available at http://gmaildefault.codeplex.com. Simply run the free program and choose Google Apps (i.e., not "Gmail") as your default e-mail service:

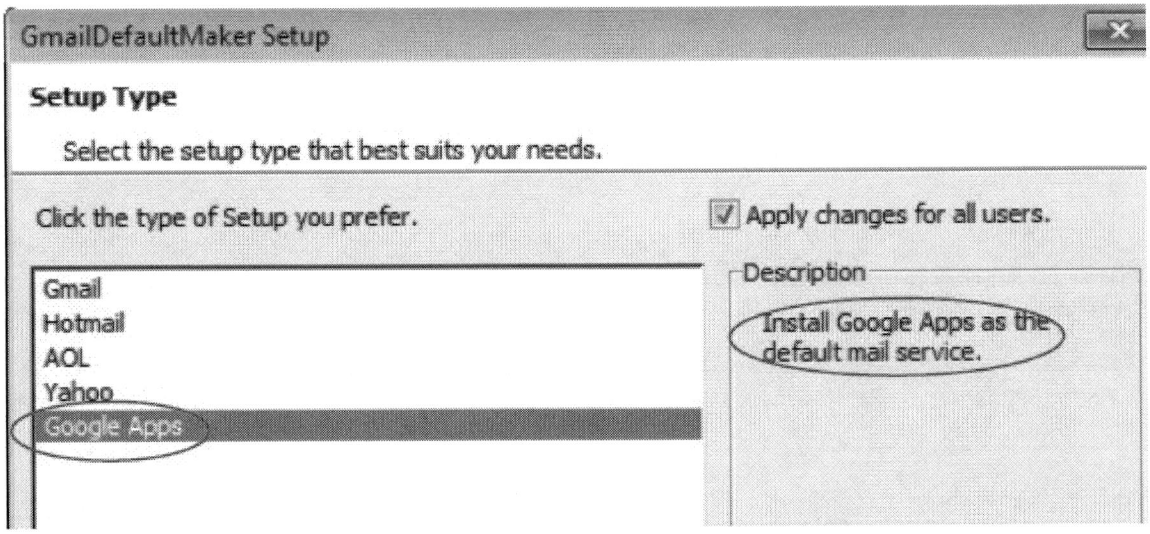

Now, whenever you click a "mailto" link, Windows will open a compose mail window linked to your Gmail for Business account.

III. GOOGLE CALENDAR

Google Calendar is the primary reason why I have never missed a filing deadline, a court appearance, or even an appointment, and is the digital heart and soul of my practice.

Google Calendar is one of the products that comes with the Google Apps for Business suite. Similar to Gmail, Google Calendar is in the Cloud, which means Google stores your digital calendar online and you can access your calendar from any device with an internet connection, including your smartphone. If you enable the "offline" feature you can view a read-only version of your calendar if you lack internet access.

Entering an event in your calendar is as simple as pointing, clicking on the appropriate date and time on your calendar, and typing event details. Google enables users to enter quite a few details for any given event:

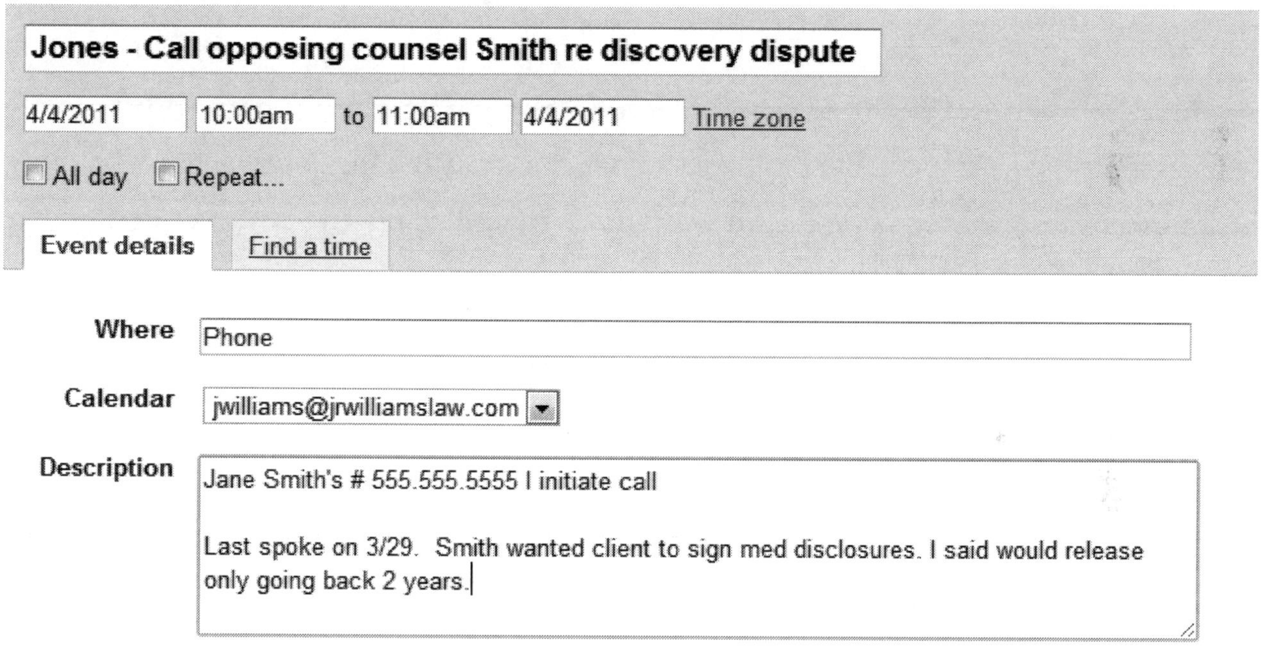

If you are familiar with Outlook, then you will feel comfortable using Google Calendar.

I generally leave my calendar open on my web browser and Google Calendar notifies me of an approaching event by opening a dialog box. Google Calendar also sends event notifications to my Gmail account and my smartphone (I will explain how to sync Gmail and Google Calendar with your smartphone in later sections of this chapter).

The following subsections highlight how to maximize Google Calendar in your practice.

A. Utilize Your Calendar

The reason why Google Calendar has helped me maintain a perfect attendance record is not because the program is particularly sophisticated, as the basic technology has been around for years. Rather, I always know what is going on in my practice because I religiously enter every event in my practice into my calendar.

When a judge issues a scheduling order, I enter every single event and deadline set forth in the order in my calendar the day the order comes out.

If opposing counsel and I conclude a conversation by agreeing to discuss settlement in one week, I "tickle" my calendar to call opposing counsel in seven days. I will include the opposing counsel's name and number in the event and note how we ended the previous conversation so we can pick up right where we left off. If I call and opposing counsel does not answer, then I drag and drop the appointment into another time slot to remember to follow up:

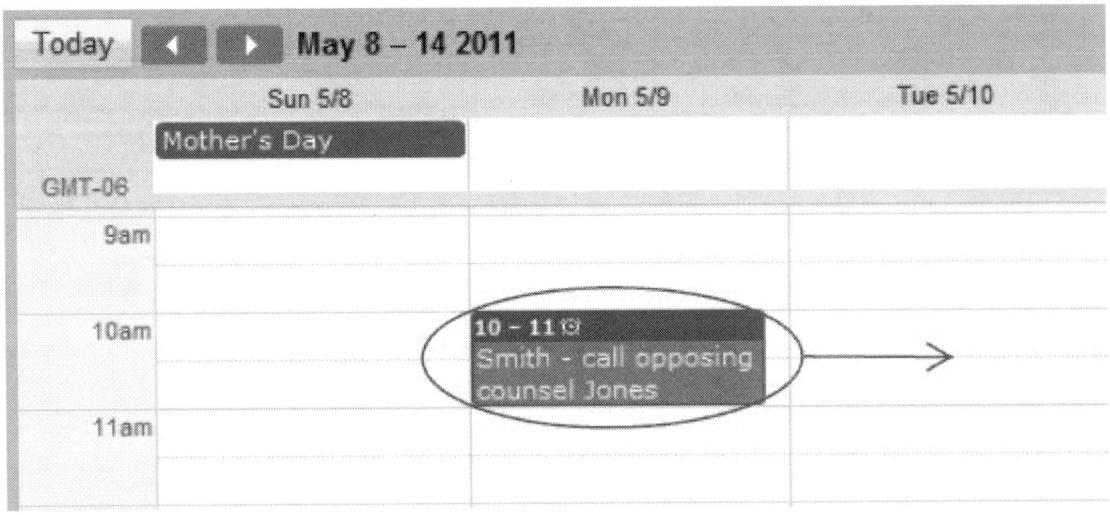

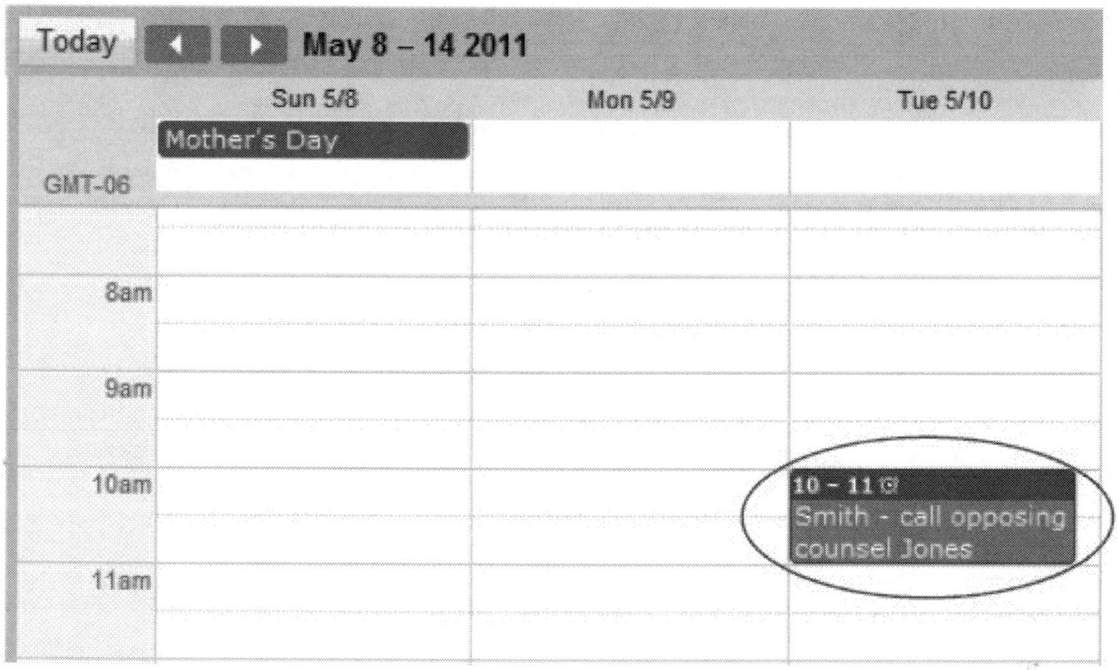

If I set an in-person interview with a potential new client, I enter the appointment into my calendar while I am on the phone setting the appointment. I will include the potential new client's phone number and a brief description of his legal issue in the calendar entry so I will remember his issue when I meet him in person:

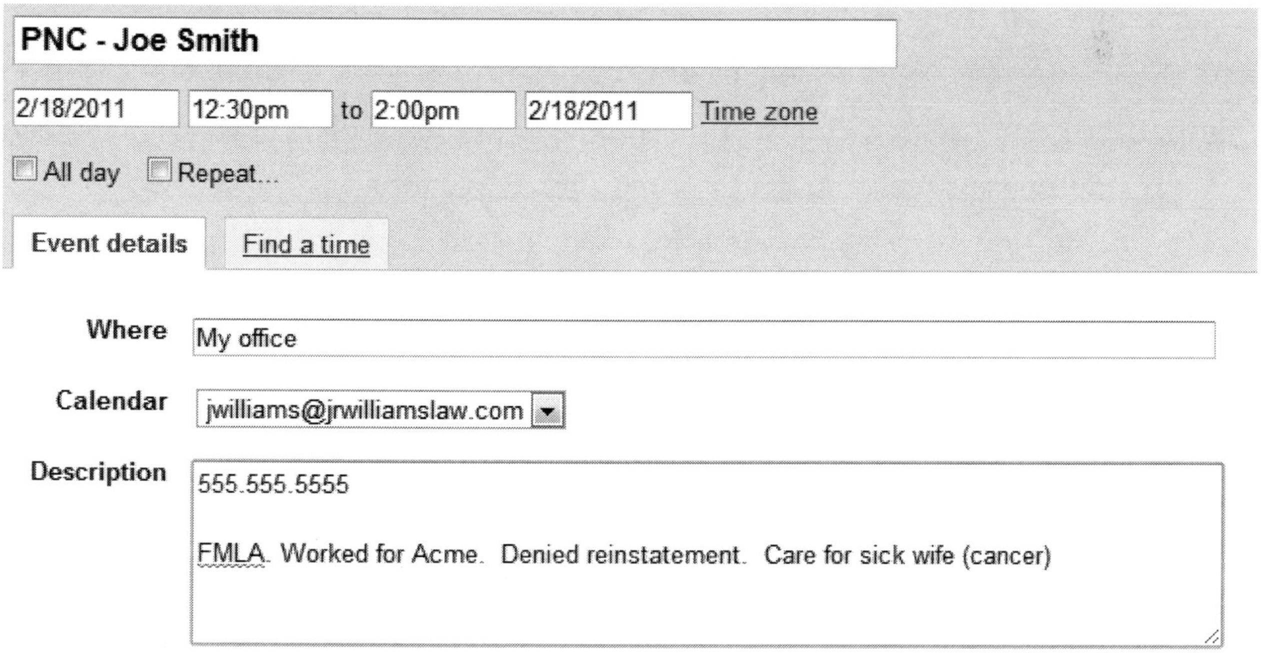

If I promise to provide opposing counsel with a draft of a document that I know will take two hours to compose, I will block off two consecutive hours on my calendar to work on the project well before the deadline to provide the draft.

If I am attending a deposition, I enter the event into my calendar and include the location's address, and if I am deposing the witness I will include my court reporter's contact information.

If I speak to a client at 3 PM and promise to call her back in an hour, I make an entry in my calendar to call her back at 4 PM just in case it slips my mind.

And so on and so forth.

By entering every event in my practice into my calendar, I avoid double booking, and can see everything that's going on in my practice just by glancing at my calendar. By entering sufficient details when I set an event, I eliminate guesswork and prepare for exigencies.

Organization is critically important to maintaining a successful solo practice. If you are unable to stay on top of things you risk, among other things, colleagues labeling you a flake and not referring clients to you; judges labeling you as unprofessional and not giving you the benefit of the doubt when you argue before them; opposing counsel refusing to take you seriously as a formidable adversary and low-balling you when you engage in settlement negotiations; and clients firing you because you fail to return their phone calls in a timely manner and never seem to know what's going on in their cases.

My calendaring system enables me to keep a handle on exactly what is going on in all my cases (I typically maintain 30-40 active cases) at all times. The life of a solo litigator can get stressful, but I am never so harried that I am unable to reply to every communication I receive (phone, fax, or e-mail) within 24 hours of receipt.

B. Search My Calendars

If I want to know all the upcoming events in a particular case, I simply enter the client's last name in the search box at the top of the screen on Google Calendar and press the "Search My Calendars" button. Google Calendar then generates every upcoming event that contains the client's last name:

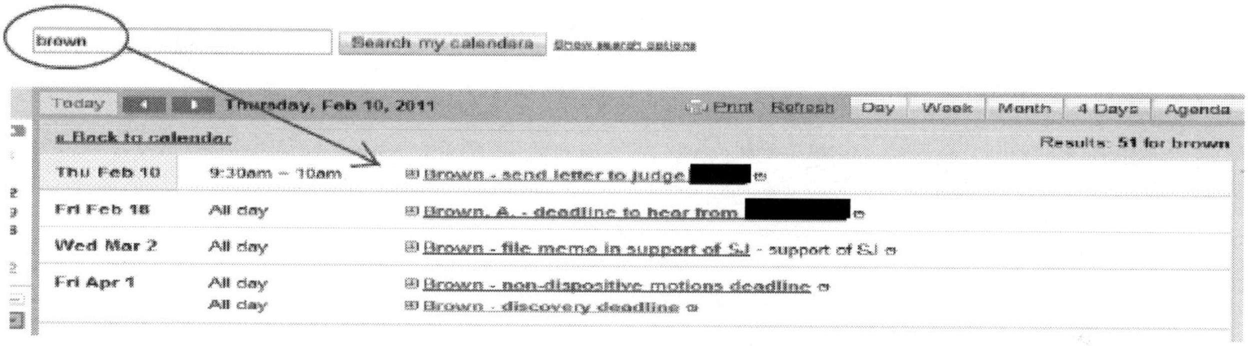

This is an effective method of getting the 30,000 foot view of any case because I always include the client's last name in calendar entries.

C. Tungle.me

Tungle.me enables potential clients to view my public calendar and set initial phone consultations online:

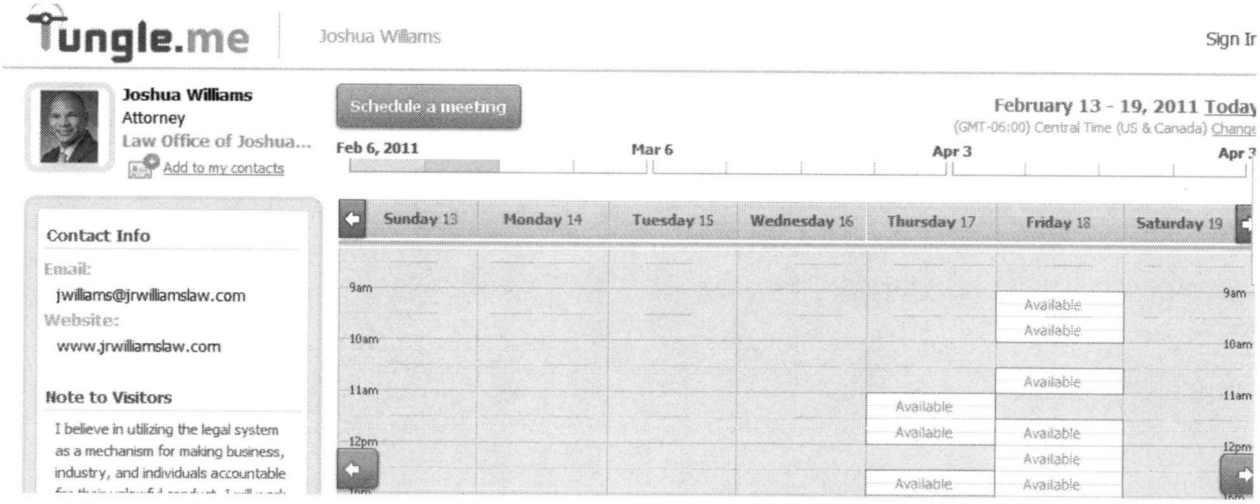

If a client sends me an e-mail inquiry, I simply reply with a canned response that includes a link to my public calendar and specific instructions on how to schedule a consultation:

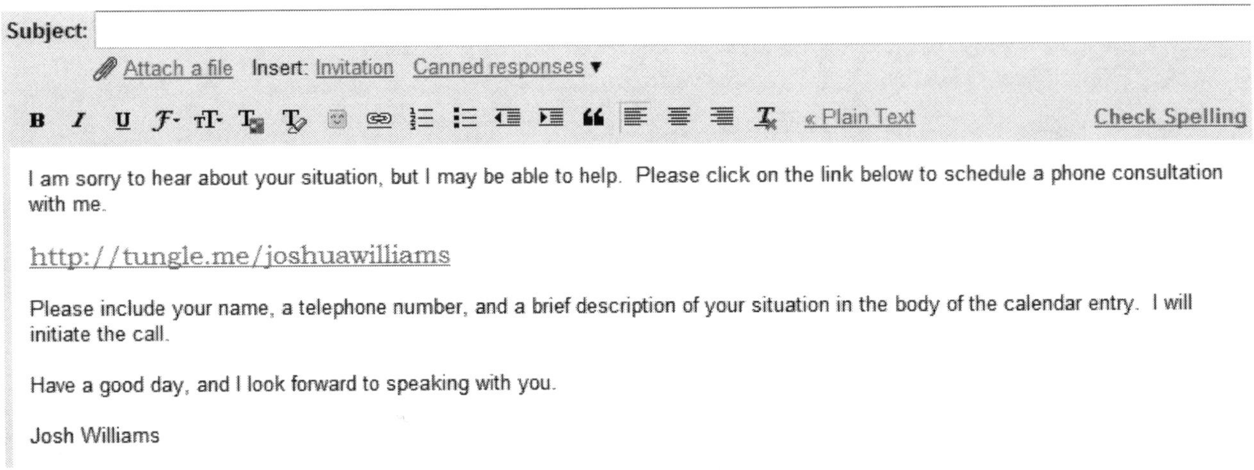
Subject:

Attach a file Insert: Invitation Canned responses ▾

« Plain Text Check Spelling

I am sorry to hear about your situation, but I may be able to help. Please click on the link below to schedule a phone consultation with me.

http://tungle.me/joshuawilliams

Please include your name, a telephone number, and a brief description of your situation in the body of the calendar entry. I will initiate the call.

Have a good day, and I look forward to speaking with you.

Josh Williams

Every page of my firm's website features a "Schedule a Free Consultation" button that links to a page that contains a link to my public calendar and instructions on how to schedule a consultation:

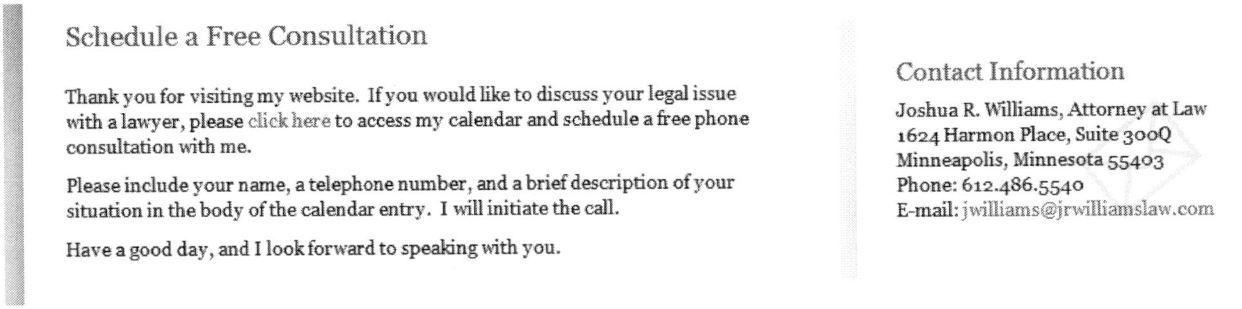
Schedule a Free Consultation

Thank you for visiting my website. If you would like to discuss your legal issue with a lawyer, please click here to access my calendar and schedule a free phone consultation with me.

Please include your name, a telephone number, and a brief description of your situation in the body of the calendar entry. I will initiate the call.

Have a good day, and I look forward to speaking with you.

Contact Information

Joshua R. Williams, Attorney at Law
1624 Harmon Place, Suite 300Q
Minneapolis, Minnesota 55403
Phone: 612.486.5540
E-mail: jwilliams@jrwilliamslaw.com

Tungle.me, available at tungle.me/Home, is completely free, and helps me capture at least one new client every two months that would otherwise slip through the cracks. Considering my average case is worth about $5,000 in fees (including cases where I get "zeroed out"), Tungle.me makes me roughly $30,000 a year.

IV. WEB BROWSER: GOOGLE CHROME

A web browser is the program you use to access the Internet. Windows Internet Explorer and Mozilla Firefox were the most popular browsers for PC users for many years, but I urge you to download Google Chrome (available at http://www.google.com/chrome), which I believe is the superior program. Before Chrome came out I used Firefox instead of Explorer because Firefox was just as fast as Explorer and more secure. Web browser speed is crucial to my practice because I use multiple software programs in the Cloud, rather than programs installed on a computer's hard drive. Chrome is even faster than Firefox and no less secure, and because I was not a huge fan of the bloated Firefox interface I made the switch to Chrome.

The following subsections highlight features within Chrome that I frequently utilize in my practice.

A. Tabbed Browsing

Tabbed browsing enables Chrome users to keep several webpages open within a single web browser window by clicking on tabs at the top of the web browser. Wisegeek.com explains how tabbed browsing works:

> Tabs appear in the browser window when more than one webpage is opened. Each open webpage has its own tab, with the active tab displaying its page "up front," the inactive tabs hidden behind. By clicking on a tab the user switches that page up front for quick viewing.
>
> Tabbed browsing is extremely useful in a variety of situations. If you are reading a webpage and would like to click a link without losing your place, you can open the link in a tabbed window. After reading the link you can close the tab or just click on the original tab to switch back to the previous page, keeping both pages available. Tabbed browsing eliminates the need to repeatedly reload pages or use the "back" button.

I generally keep tabs for the webpages I use most often—Gmail, Calendar, Westlaw, Google Scholar, and Bill4Time—active at all times:

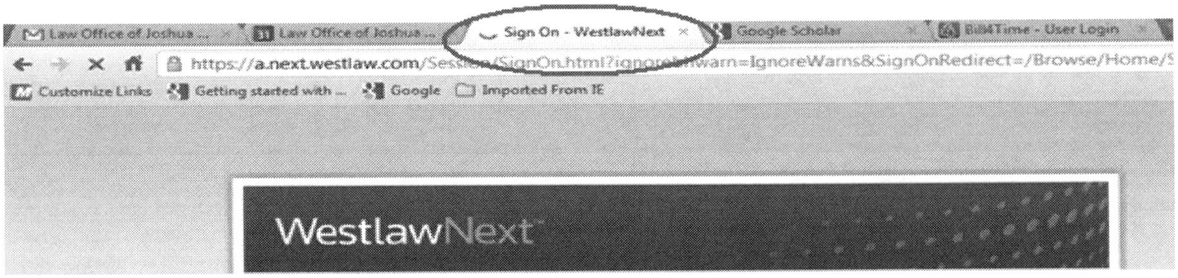

B. Bookmarks

Bookmarks, called "Favorites" in Explorer, enable Chrome users to quickly access frequently visited pages with a single click. Bookmarks are important to my practice because I frequently use Cloud applications rather than programs installed on my computer's hard drive:

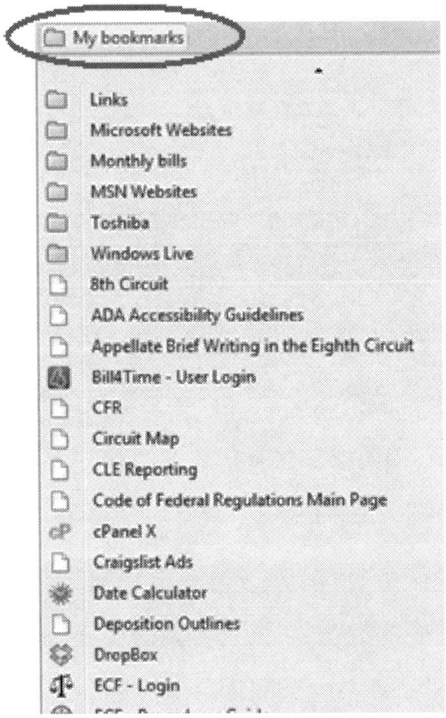

If you have been using Explorer or Firefox as your browser, visit http://tinyurl.com/4yprrl for information on how to easily import your existing favorites/bookmarks into Chrome.

C. Chrome Sync

Chrome Sync enables users to sync browser settings with any computer they are using. Thus, when I sign in to my Google account from any computer in the world with an internet connection, my Chrome settings—including all my bookmarks—are the same as if I was using my office computer. As I discussed in Chapter 1, I use multiple computers in my practice, and not having to create new bookmarks on every computer I use saves me considerable time and hassle. Visit http://tinyurl.com/2bcad98 for information on how to enable Sync.

V. PHONE SYSTEM

My phone system is one of the most low-tech systems I use in my practice, but it is highly efficient. The following subsections describe the different components of my phone system.

A. Virtual Receptionist

The nature of my practice, unfortunately, is that only about one out of every 25-30 potential clients I come in contact with has a viable claim. Given that most potential clients use the phone to initiate contact with me, I need to field a lot of calls in order to find clients. At this early stage in my solo career, the majority of potential clients who call me find out about my firm via the internet. Thus, unlike referrals who will wait for me to call back if I am not available when they call, most potential clients who call me will just hang up and call the next lawyer on the list if a live voice does not pick up.

For obvious reasons I cannot answer every call I receive, and hiring a receptionist to answer my phone was cost prohibitive. Listening to voice mails and playing phone tag with potential clients who actually took the time to leave messages (and colleagues, clerks, and other persons who call me) took up hours of my precious time each week.

The solution: Total Attorneys' Virtual Receptionist (visit www.totalattorneys.com).

Total Attorneys provides attorneys with several options for using its virtual receptionist service, including an option where attorneys can route all incoming calls to a virtual receptionist ("VR"). I prefer answering my own phone (and do not believe doing so undermines my professionalism in any way), thus I have configured my virtual receptionist service as follows:

1. If I do not pick up my phone after four rings, my phone company (at my request) routes calls to the VR call center in Chicago.
2. The VR—a real person—will greet clients with "Law Office of Joshua R. Williams, how may I help you?" A VR will answer my phone 24 hours a day, seven days a week.
3. If the caller is anyone other than a potential new client (and calls during business hours), the VR will call my smartphone. If I answer, the VR will tell me who is on the other line. If I want to speak with the caller, the VR will connect the call. If I do not answer or if I instruct the VR to not connect the call (or if the call is after business hours), the VR will take a message and will immediately send me the message via e-mail:

New message from 'Attorney Kevin [redacted]

virtualreceptionist@totalattorneys.com to me — show details 3:33 PM (1 hour

total attorneys™

Joshua Williams,

You have a new message:

name	Attorney Kevin [redacted]
home phone	
cell phone	(507) [redacted]
office phone	
email address	
time	Fri, Feb 18 @ 03:30 PM CT
receptionist	Kevin B
activity	Attempted to Connect Call
notes	Mr. [redacted] said he was calling about two cases: a common one and one he would like to refer to Mr. Williams. Mr. Williams was unavailable. Mr. [redacted] would like a call back.

Thus, if I am on the go I can check all my messages instantly from my smartphone. If I am away from the office for a day or more, I do not need to set aside hours to listen to voicemails, but can easily find out who called me by simply checking my Gmail inbox.

4. If the caller is a potential new client, the VR will access my public Google Calendar and set an initial phone consultation:

New message from 'Sara [redacted] Potential Client'

virtualreceptionist@totalattorneys.com to me — show details 9:43 AM (7 h

total attorneys™

Joshua Williams,

You have a new message:

name	Sara [redacted] - Potential Client
home phone	
cell phone	(651) [redacted]
office phone	
email address	[redacted]@aol.com
time	Fri, Feb 18 @ 09:39 AM CT
receptionist	David A
activity	Took Message
notes	Scheduled an initial consultation for an Employment Law situation for Wednesday, 2/23, at 10am.

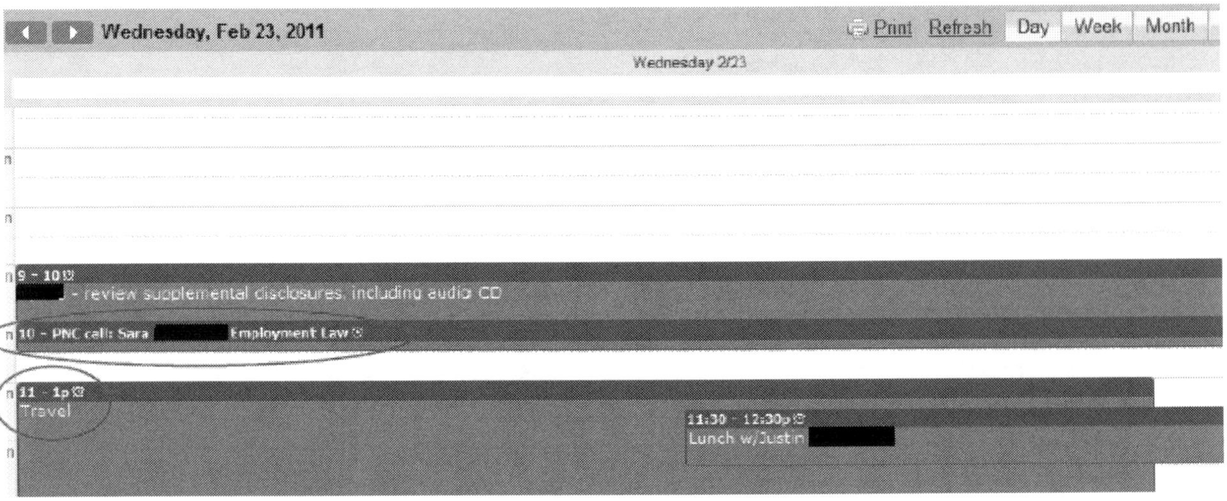

The appointment setting feature obviates the need to engage in seemingly endless games of telephone tag with clients. An initial problem with the feature was that the VRs were setting appointments when I was in-transit, but I solved this problem by entering travel time in my calendar entries (see graphic above).

I should note that roughly 30 percent of potential new clients who set initial phone consultations with the VR do not answer when I call back at the arranged time, but if a potential client cannot remember a simple phone consultation, then s/he probably isn't going to be a good client anyway. Thus, an unintended benefit of the appointment setting feature is that it weeds out "bad" clients.

Total Attorneys' Virtual Receptionist is the most important tool in my practice from a psychological standpoint because it alleviates my compulsion to answer *every* call I receive. Rather, if I am engaged in another activity, I can rest assured that someone will take a message, promptly relay the message via e-mail, and set an appointment when appropriate. My VR service costs between $150 and $200 per month, depending on how many calls I receive.

The VR service is not without its problems, as the service is somewhat impersonal because the VRs only know basic information about me and my practice. While it would be nice to have a dedicated, in-house receptionist who could provide lost clients with directions to my office or let opposing counsel know I will not be able to return her call because I am stuck in depositions all day, my level of satisfaction with the VR service is high enough that I do not feel compelled to pay an additional $30,000 to $40,000 per year for the personal touch.

The VRs botch an occasional message or appointment, but probably not at a higher rate than an in-house receptionist would.

Finally, I should note that my office is located in a building with about a dozen tenants who share a receptionist. The receptionist, who is very friendly and highly competent, greets all my in-person appointments, and between visits from opposing counsel, client meetings, depositions, mediations, etc., I receive enough office visitors that I would need to hire a full-time in-house receptionist if I did not benefit from the shared receptionist's services.

B. <u>Cordless Phone System</u>

I spend so much time on the phone in my practice that I was going through at least one phone cord a month. To remedy this problem, I purchased an AT&T cordless phone network, which is made up of one base station that is connected to the phone jack and additional handsets that do not require a jack:

AT&T Cordless Phone Network

I keep the base unit in my office, set up one of the additional handsets in the workspace outside my office for my law clerk to use, and use the third handset as a backup. I purchased the network for about $70 at Office Max.

C. <u>Landline and High-Speed Internet</u>

My landlord only allows its tenants to use a certain phone company for phone and internet service. My phone line is analog and I pay about $25 each month for unlimited local calling and caller ID and about $15 each month for long-distance calls at five cents a minute. I pay about $40 each month for high-speed internet. I should note that solos need high-speed internet connectivity because a dial-up connection is way too slow. If your landlord does not provide free high-speed internet or compel you to use a provider of his or her choosing, your local phone or cable company can provide service for about $40 per month.

If I made more long-distance calls I would be very tempted to transfer my phone number to Vonage, which is a VoIP (Voice over Internet Protocol) phone system. Vonage works by connecting a phone adapter to your high-speed internet connection and connecting your phone to the adapter. Vonage offers "Cadillac" plans with all the bells and whistles (caller ID, unlimited long distance, three-way calling, etc.) for about $50 a month.

Finally, if I did not run a high-volume practice where it is essential that every potential new client who calls me gets a live voice and can set an appointment, I would probably find a way to utilize Google Voice. Google Voice, among other things, provides free long-distance calling and a single 10-digit phone number for all your mobile, home, and work numbers. Thus, when someone calls your Google Voice number, all your phones ring simultaneously (note: Vonage also offers subscribers this feature up to five phone numbers). Given that I already use a virtual receptionist to answer any phone calls I can't answer myself and the VR will connect such calls to my smartphone, Google Voice doesn't really fit into my practice. Visit http://tinyurl.com/ylmsl43 to learn about all the features Google Voice offers and download the program for free.

D. Smartphone

A smartphone is a mobile phone that offers greater internet connectivity and computing ability compared to a regular mobile phone. The three smartphone market leaders are iPhones, Blackberrys, and phones that run on Google's Android operating system. These days any smartphone application you could possibly want to use in your practice is compatible with all three market leaders, so there is no inherent advantage in choosing one style of phone over another.

The model I use is the Blackberry Pearl Flip 8220:

Blackberry Pearl Flip 8220

I do not particularly care for the Pearl, as it frequently malfunctions in a variety of ways, does not feature a full QWERTY keypad, and runs on the EDGE network, so its internet connectivity is much slower than phones that run on 3G or 4G networks. As much as I would like to upgrade to a newer phone, I am reluctant to ditch the Pearl because I prefer the flip style and do not care for the touchscreen style of Android and iPhones. Blackberry did come out with an updated flip phone that features a QWERTY keypad and runs on the 3G network—the Style 9670—but Sprint is the only carrier that supports the Style. I do not want to switch carriers because I believe my carrier, T-Mobile, provides superior service in my part of the country.

I should note that I fully acknowledge my preference for flip phones is very 2006, and when I take out my Pearl in business settings people's perception is often that I am behind the technological times. Given that it looks like flip phones are going the way of the dodo, I will probably break down and upgrade my phone in the next few months. I will likely purchase another Blackberry device because I am comfortable with the Blackberry interface and do not believe iPhones or Android devices are superior business products.

Regardless of what model you select, solos must purchase smartphones to stay on top of things in their practices. If you do not like giving clients and colleagues implicit access to you at all times via your smartphone, then you are probably not cut out for solo practice. That said, I do recommend setting boundaries to protect against burnout. In my case, I generally do not answer my phone after business hours, I refuse to check my Blackberry during meals, and I ration my Blackberry use during vacation and family time.

You can purchase a new smartphone for around $100. I highly recommend you sign up for a monthly service plan with unlimited data usage, which costs about $100 per month.

The following subsections highlight the most important applications and features I use on my smartphone.

1. Google Mobile Apps

Google Mobile Apps refers to several applications that bring Google to your smartphone. The Google Mobile applications most important to my practice are Gmail Mobile and Google Sync. Gmail Mobile enables users to read and send e-mails from your smartphone, and Google Sync automatically synchronizes your Google Calendar and contacts to your smartphone. Thus, no matter where I am in the world, I always have access to my e-mail and updated calendar.

Visit http://www.google.com/mobile for information on how to download Google Mobile Apps for free.

2. Documents To Go

Certain e-mail attachments did not open properly or did not open at all from my smartphone, which often frustrated my ability to get work done on the go. If you download Documents To Go on your smartphone, any Word, Excel, PowerPoint, or PDF file will open properly from your mobile device. Documents To Go also enables users to edit and create Word, Excel, PowerPoint, and PDF files from their smartphones. Visit www.dataviz.com to download Documents To Go for about $15.

3. Dropbox

In Chapter 3 I will discuss how I use Dropbox to synchronize all my digital files between computers and access my files from any computer with an internet connection. The Dropbox mobile application enables me to access every file in my practice from my smartphone. Used in tandem with Documents To Go, the Dropbox mobile application also enables users to edit and create documents from their smartphones and sync such documents with any device linked to their Dropbox account.

Visit http://www.dropbox.com/anywhere to download the Dropbox mobile application for free.

4. Tethering

Tethering enables smartphone users to access the internet from their laptop computers by using their smartphones as a modem via USB cable or bluetooth:

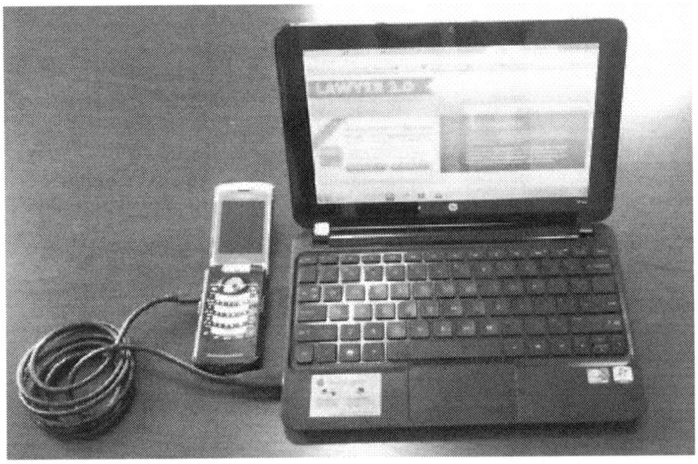

Tethering Smartphone to Netbook

Tethering comes in extremely handy when I am on the go and there are no wi-fi hotspots available, or if my internet connection at my office goes down. I tether my computer to my smartphone often enough that I would probably pay for mobile broadband service (about $50 per month from T-Mobile) if the tethering feature was not available.

The two main drawbacks to tethering are (1) if your smartphone runs on anything less than 3G speeds your internet connection is going to be rather slow, and (2) some wireless carriers do not allow tethering or charge a steep fee, even if you pay for an unlimited data plan.

Visit http://tinyurl.com/27ovdyz for information on how to tether your smartphone to your computer on AT&T, Verizon, Sprint, and T-Mobile networks.

VI. CASE MANAGEMENT SOFTWARE

Case management software refers generally to stand-alone, jack-of-all-trade programs that keep track of and manage case information. There are many programs available, and each offers different features and functions such as calendaring, contact management, time and billing, accounting, document management, etc. I do not need case management software for contact management and calendaring because I use Gmail and Google Calendar to perform these functions. Additionally, I do not need case management software to include document management features because, as set forth in Chapter 3, I use the Windows folder system for document management.

I need my case management software to perform the following functions: track time, track expenses, track accounting, track trust accounting, generate invoices, and serve as a central database for case and client information. I also wanted to use a case management program that is software as a service (SaaS), which refers to web-based software that users can access from any computer with an internet connection.

I selected Bill4Time (available at www.bill4time.com) as my case management software because, at the time I launched my firm in Fall 2009, it was the only case management SaaS that offered all the features I was looking for (Rocket Matter offered everything except trust accounting management). While Bill4Time does everything I need it to do, it does not do anything particularly well; using Bill4Time reminds me of the Marie Callender frozen meals I survived on back in the early 2000s in that the user experience is a step up from awful yet far from satisfying. Specifically, the interface is clunky, features that should be simple feel bloated, features that should be robust feel too thin, and nothing about the program is intuitive. Basically, Bill4Time is just like an Apple product, only the exact opposite.

Even though Bill4Time comes up short, I do not feel compelled to upgrade my case management software because the nature of my practice does not require me to utilize the product extensively. To clarify, I work almost all my cases under contingency fee arrangements, which means I rarely need to enter payments received (i.e., a few times each month in a good month), track accounting, or generate invoices. While I do keep track of my hours, I do not need to slavishly track hours as if I used the billable hour business model.

I primarily use Bill4Time to serve as a central database for all my cases and to track time and expenses, and Bill4Time performs these functions reasonably well. This is what my Bill4Time dashboard looks like:

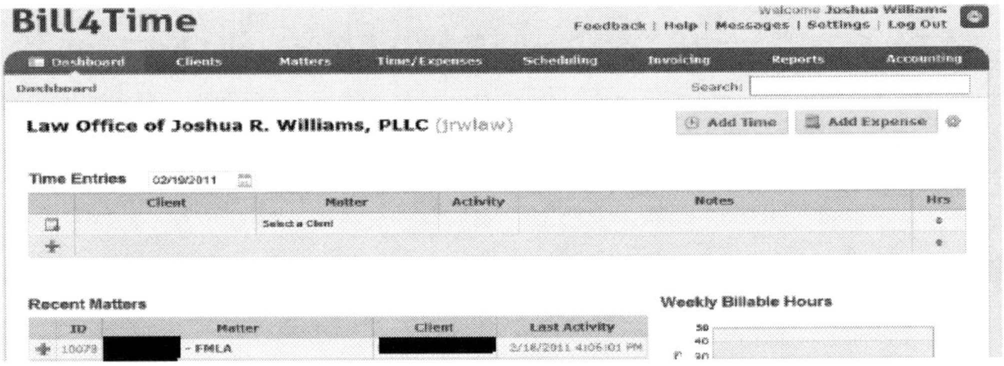

Bill4Time charges $39.99 per month for each unique user.

If I was starting a new firm today I would probably select Rocket Matter (available at www.rocketmatter.com) as my case management SaaS. Rocket Matter has received rave reviews and added a trust accounting feature in Spring 2010. Rocket Matter charges $59.99 per month for each unique user. Although I am tempted to switch to Rocket Matter, I doubt I will do so because Bill4Time's performance is satisfactory with respect to the features I use regularly in my practice, and exporting all my existing data from Bill4Time to Rocket Matter seems like an administrative nightmare. If I used the invoicing and accounting features more often, I would switch to Rocket Matter because Bill4Time performs these functions so poorly.

Thus, my final verdict is that I tepidly endorse Bill4Time as a low-cost case management SaaS if you work most cases under contingency or flat-fee arrangements. Otherwise, I recommend Rocket Matter.

Finally, I highly recommend that solos use SaaS case management software because SaaS obviates the need to install the software on every computer you use in your practice and negates the need to perform software updates. Moreover, if your computer is stolen or crashes, you can access your updated case information—and the latest version of the software—from a replacement machine simply by logging into your account via the internet.

VII. POSTAGE AND LABELING

As I discussed in Chapter 1, I use the Dymo Labelwriter 450 Twin Turbo for postage and labeling.

VIII. INTERNET FAX SERVICE

There is no good reason why anyone should still send documents via fax given that virtually all e-mail clients enable users to send documents via e-mail as attachments. Unfortunately, many courts, clients, and colleagues still insist on sending and receiving documents via fax, thus every solo needs fax capabilities.

I highly recommend using MaxEmail (available at www.maxemail.com) to send and receive faxes via e-mail. When users sign up for an account, MaxEmail assigns a unique 10-digit fax number. When someone faxes documents to your fax number, MaxEmail delivers the documents as PDF attachments via e-mail:

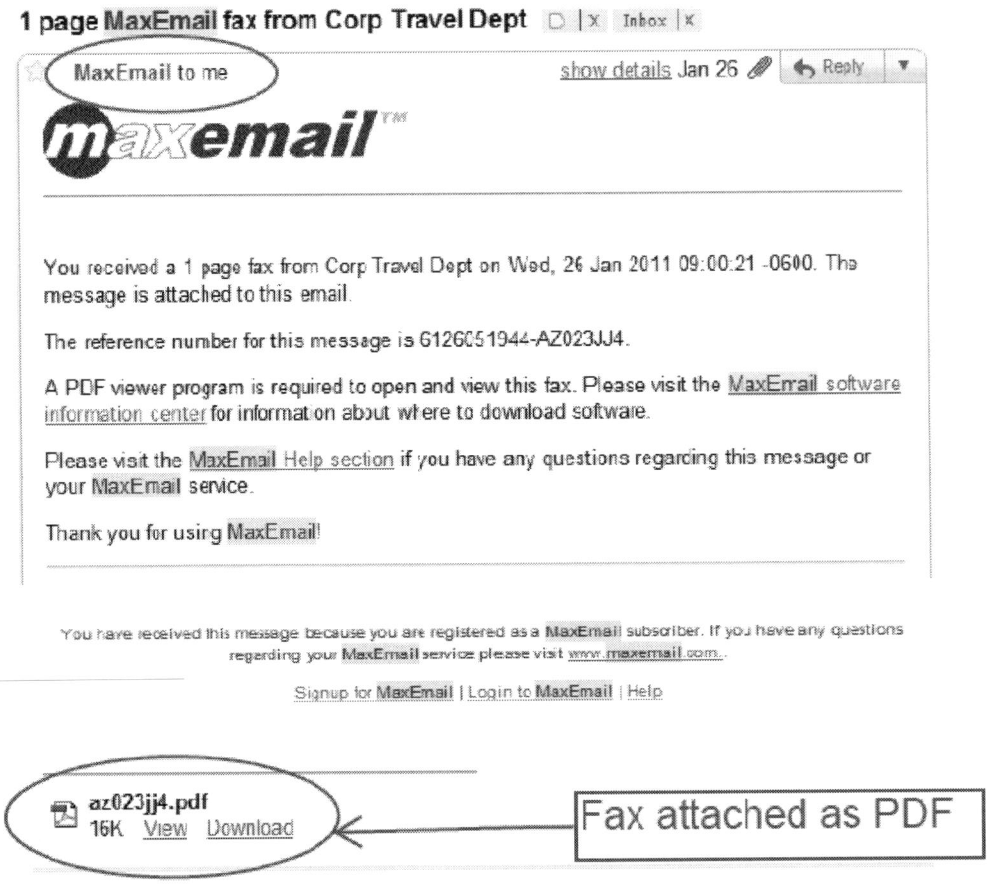

To send a fax, simply address an e-mail to [*recipient's fax number*]@maxemailsend.com, attach any files (Word, PDF, Excel, etc.) you want the recipient to receive, and press send. Alternatively, you can use MaxEmail's web interface to send faxes.

MaxEmail charges only $9.95 per month for 250 inbound pages and 100 outbound pages. Additional pages cost five cents per page (I rarely exceed my monthly quotas).

MaxEmail is much cheaper and more efficient than a traditional fax machine. If you are reluctant to give up your traditional fax machine because you want to retain the ability to fax hard copies of documents, I will alleviate your concerns in the next chapter by showing you how to easily convert hard copies of documents into digital files.

IX. LETTERHEAD AND LOGO

The Biglaw firm I worked at used fancy pre-printed letterhead, and every time lawyers wanted to send out a letter we (and by "we" I mean support staff) had to manually load the fancy letterhead into printers. As a busy solo, I do not have time to manually load pre-printed letterhead every time I need to print a letter, and I do not want to pay for letterhead, which can get pricey. Additionally, I send most letters electronically, and feeding a printer with pre-printed letterhead, printing the letter, and scanning the final product onto my hard drive so I can send the letter as an e-mail attachment is highly inefficient. My simple solution was to create my own letterhead on my word processing software, Microsoft Word:

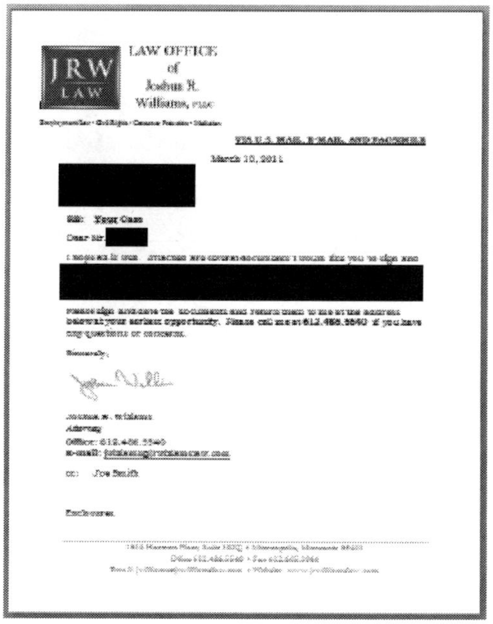
JRW LAW

LAW OFFICE
of
Joshua R.
Williams, PLLC

March 10, 2011

[redacted]

Dear Mr. [redacted]

[redacted]

Sincerely,

cc: Joe Smith

Enclosures

I save the document in a Windows folder (I will explain how Windows folders work in Chapter 3) where I store frequently-used documents and use it as a template whenever I need to compose a letter. If I want to send the letter electronically, I simply save the document as a PDF file and attach it to an e-mail:

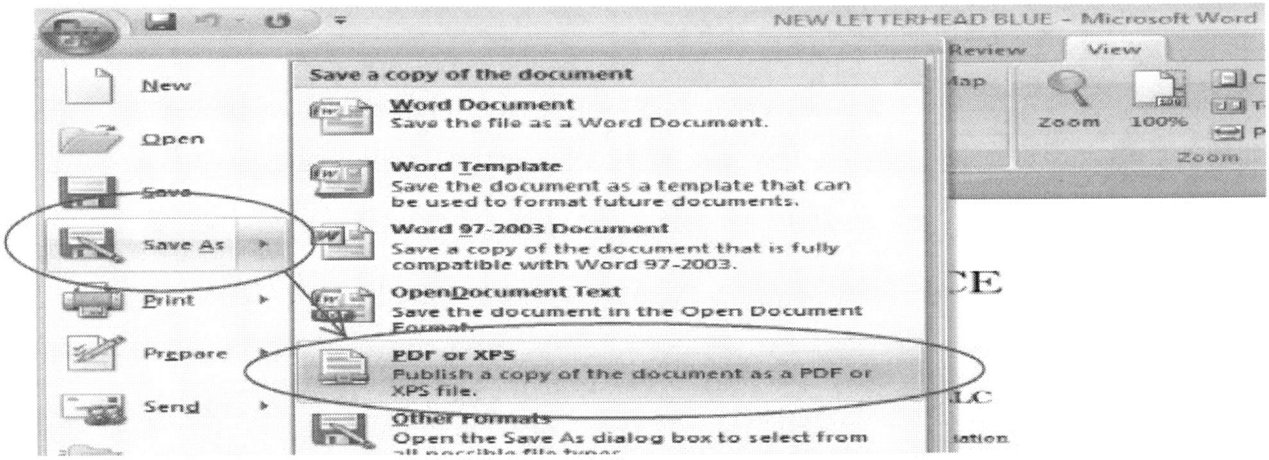

If you think creating your own letterhead on Word is beyond the scope of what you can do on your own, it's not. Visit http://tinyurl.com/4oopj2z to access over 100 letterhead templates that are available to download for free from Microsoft.

I wanted a custom logo for my letterhead because I think it looks cool, clean and professional. I recommend using Robert Pufahl of RP Printworks Design (visit www.rpprintworksdesign.com to view his online portfolio and contact information) to design your custom logo. You can call Robert from anywhere in the country, tell him what you are looking for, and he will provide you with several custom logo options to choose from for a very reasonable price. I should note that Robert designed the cover of this book as well as my firm logo.

Finally, please note that in order to print color copies you will, of course, need a color printer. As I discussed in Chapter 1, I recommend the HP Officejet Pro 8500.

X. BACKUP SYSTEM

You need to back up your files. If you have a paperless office like me and convert any hard copies of documents you receive into digital files and shred the originals, you *really* need to back up your files. For ethical and practical reasons, you cannot simply rely on saving your files to your computer's hard drive.

Even though I fully appreciate the importance of backing up data, I hate doing it. Specifically, I do not like having to take the time to manually back up my files. Thus, I wanted a backup system that backed up my files automatically without me having to think about it. Additionally, I wanted a product that would back up my files offsite to protect against theft, fire, spills, etc.

The following subsections describe the tools I use to back up my files.

A. Seagate Replica

As I discussed in Chapter 1, I use the Seagate Replica as my onsite backup solution. The Replica is an external hard drive that automatically backs up your computer's hard drive when you plug it into your computer via USB cable. Every time you add or modify your hard drive, the Replica automatically captures the modification.

B. Carbonite

The Replica is a fine piece of equipment, but if someone stole the device from my office or if it was damaged beyond repair I would not be able to access my backed up files. I did not want to take the Replica home with me every night because doing so would be a hassle and I was afraid the device might get lost or damaged in transit.

Carbonite, available for download at www.carbonite.com, is an online backup service that backs up users' files on remote servers. Any time users create new files or modify existing ones, Carbonite automatically sends encrypted copies of those files over your high-speed internet connection to secure, remote servers. When you need to retrieve your files, the Carbonite software quickly restores your files to the correct location on your original computer or on a replacement machine. You can also access your backed up files from any device with an internet connection.

Carbonite will not back up your files unless your computer is connected to the internet. Once your computer regains internet connectivity, Carbonite automatically backs up any new or modified files.

A one-year Carbonite subscription costs $54.95 and provides unlimited backup storage.

C. Dropbox

I will discuss Dropbox in greater detail in Chapter 3 and limit the scope of this subsection to how this elegant program supplements my backup system. Dropbox is an online backup service that offers all the same features as Carbonite and the same level of security. Dropbox is not merely redundant of Carbonite, as it also automatically syncs files across your office computers. Thus, every time I add or modify files on one of my office computers, the addition or modification is automatically backed up in at least five locations: (1) my laptop's hard drive, (2) my netbook's hard drive, (3) Carbonite, (4) Dropbox, and (5) my Replica. Accordingly, I am not concerned about losing a file.

Finally, online backup systems are secure. As I discussed earlier in this chapter, I concede that a highly motivated hacker could hack into Dropbox's or Carbonite's secure remote servers, but a semi-motivated common thief could break into your office and steal your firm's server, your computer, or hard copies of your client files if you refuse to go paperless.

Dropbox provides 2 GB of storage for free, 50 GB for $99 per year, and 100 GB for $199 per year.

LAWYER 2.0 The Paperless Law Office

I. INTRODUCTION

Going paperless has been such an integral part of building a sustainable six-figure practice that I felt compelled to devote an entire chapter of this book to the subject. Quite simply, my decision to go paperless is the main reason why I am able to compete with more established attorneys for business and serve as a worthy adversary to the largest firms in the Midwest.

As I discussed in Chapter 1, the term "paperless law office" is a misnomer, as it is not possible for lawyers to completely eschew paper documents. While I convert every document that comes into my office into a digital file, I still need to print hard copies of documents on a regular basis. Additionally, some lawyers need to retain hard copies of certain documents (e.g., wills) for ethical or statutory purposes.

Thus, it is more accurate to say that I maintain a *digital* law office, but for organization and clarity I will use the terms "digital" and "paperless" interchangeably in this chapter.

II. ETHICAL CONCERNS AND PSYCHOLOGICAL BARRIERS

I know some lawyers who are resistant to going paperless because they believe the Rules of Conduct bar them from doing so.

I do not believe lawyers who implement my paperless system (and refrain from disabling password protection on their computers) will expose themselves to violations of Rule 1.6, which governs client confidentiality. As I have already stated several times in this book, a thief could steal your paper files more easily than he could hack into remote servers.

Additionally, I do not believe lawyers who implement my paperless system will expose themselves to violations of Rules 1.15 and 1.16, which require attorneys to properly maintain client files and deliver files to clients upon termination of representation (although some lawyers need to retain hard copies of certain documents for ethical or statutory purposes). In fact, going paperless will *help* lawyers comply with Rules 1.15 and 1.16 in the event of vandalism or *force majeure.*

Some lawyers are resistant to going paperless because they fear getting sued and needing an original document that was scanned and shredded. I doubt that such a situation is even remotely likely to happen, and even if it did you can always print out a perfect copy of the original that can be authenticated.

Finally, some lawyers do not attempt to implement a digital law office because they feel they lack requisite technological know-how. I can assure you that you do not need much technological savvy to implement a paperless office; all you need are basic computer skills and a high-speed internet connection.

III. REASONS TO GO PAPERLESS

Steve Best and Debbie Foster succinctly describe a paperless law office in their January 2009 *Practice Today* article, available at http://tinyurl.com/4ntmmtj, as "a philosophy to work with minimal paper and convert all forms of documentation into a digital form." The following subsections highlight the benefits of going paperless.

A. <u>Save Space and Reduce Clutter</u>

If I said that the main reasons why I decided to go paperless were to benefit the environment and to increase efficiency, I would be lying. In fact, the main reason why I decided to go paperless was because my first office was located in a glorified cubby hole and I lacked the space to maintain physical files. Thus, I *had* to go paperless in order to comply with the Rules of Conduct.

Since I launched my firm in Fall 2009, I have worked on over 80 cases that have generated well over 2 GB of electronic information, mostly contained in Word or PDF files. This amount of data translates into roughly 140,000 to 160,000 text pages, or 70 to 80 banker's boxes (at 2,000 pages per box), according to the Sigmund Technology Group (www.sigmundtech.com), a firm that specializes in e-discovery and computer forensics. Even though my practice generates a huge amount of data, the only dedicated physical storage repository I use is a half-empty file cabinet.

I rarely give thought to how much physical space I save by virtue of running a paperless law office; it's just how I operate. In February 2011, I inherited a civil rights case from one of the largest firms in the state that underscored how important maintaining a digital office is to saving space. The fact pattern in the case was not particularly complex, discovery was not extensive, and motion practice did not produce many exhibits. Even though the litigants did not engage in protracted litigation, the size of the physical file was two full banker's boxes. If I operated like a large firm and maintained such unwieldy physical files I would run out of storage space in a matter of months.

My workspace is not littered with bulky accordion files haphazardly strewn about on my desk and floor (i.e., unlike 80 percent of individual attorney law offices I have ventured into) because my client files take up little or zero physical space. Some lawyers sunnily refer to their messy offices as "organized chaos," but when my workspace is messy it is a good indicator that I am not operating efficiently or effectively. If you implement a paperless office you will dramatically reduce clutter and find that your workspace is a more conducive place for getting things done.

B. Reduce Your Carbon Footprint

Even though saving the environment wasn't the primary reason why I decided to go paperless, it makes me feel good to know that I probably use about 90 percent less paper than I would if I ran a non-paperless office.

C. Save Money

As David Morse noted in his September 2009 *Practice Today* article, available at http://tinyurl.com/4w68rdq, going paperless enables lawyers to "save money on paper, letterhead, envelopes, exhibit tabs, postage, employee time copying and searching for documents, toner, printers, copiers, storage boxes, storage costs, and more." I can't accurately calculate how much money I save each month by running a paperless office because my office has been paperless since its inception, but I can confirm that my monthly paper and print costs are less than $20.

D. Improve Efficiency and Organization

When I worked at a Biglaw firm, people were always literally running around the office looking for client files or portions of files, including me. David Morse's description of the scene at his law firm when a file went missing, as set forth in his aforementioned *Practice Today* article, is very similar to my experience working at a non-paperless office:

> I don't know about your firm, but everyday at mine, people were looking for files. While most files were put back in the large file storage laterals located throughout the office, it always seemed that the one file that one of my attorneys needed was missing. An all points bulletin was issued and everyone scrambled to find it. The file was always found, but not before losing time and greatly decreasing efficiency.

In contrast, I can access any document from any case (open or closed) from any device with an internet connection within seconds. I do not need to scramble and issue an "all points bulletin" when I want to locate a file; I simply look on my hard drive. If for some reason I do not have my laptop or netbook handy, I will access the document via my smartphone or on another device with an internet connection.

Maintaining a paperless office reduces redundancy and promotes intuitive organization within client files. In contrast, redundancy and unwieldiness are hallmarks of client files in non-paperless offices. For example, in the case I inherited from a large, non-paperless firm, many of the documents contained in the physical file were duplicative and organized in a haphazard manner.

A paperless office negates the need to reinvent the wheel. Most law firms and lawyers are technologically savvy enough to maintain a database of frequently used electronic forms, including old pleadings, to use as templates in new cases. Indeed, the Biglaw firm I worked at used a fairly advanced document management program where lawyers could locate documents saved to the system via keyword search. For example, if I wanted to locate a template to draft a complaint in a trademark case I would type in the words "complaint" and "trademark" to access every trademark complaint saved in the firm's system and view which attorney drafted the document.

When it came to legal research, however, I was constantly reinventing the wheel. Specifically, I would often find a highly relevant case or article for a research project I was working on and print a hard copy. I did not add the hard copy to the actual client file (generally located in the assigning partner's office or a storage lateral) because I rarely had access to the actual client file, as most of my assignments were discrete research projects; I did not actually "own" any cases.

I did not have enough storage space in my office at The Firm to retain hard copies of my research. Even if I had the space, there was no logical place for me to store the materials because I lacked access to client files. Accordingly, I tossed the hard copies in the recycling bin. Invariably, a different partner would assign a similar project at a later date and I would need to spend considerable time and money (both billable to the client) searching for and printing the exact same materials I had already located in the earlier case.

In my digital office, I can locate research materials saved as digital files from an old case in seconds. I get way more work done than I did at my old firm in a shorter amount of time by working smarter, not harder.

I am routinely adverse to the largest firms in the Midwest in my cases. This means that in most of my cases I am going up against a partner, an associate or two, a paralegal, and at least one legal secretary. In other words, five against one. I have never felt overmatched because I run a lean, mean, highly organized and efficient digital law office that enables me to keep up with the large firms motion for motion, document for document, blow for blow.

E. Mobility, Portability, and Collaboration

Going paperless obviates the need for lawyers to cart around boxes of documents to court appearances, meetings, and mediations. When I need to access my client files on the go, I simply bring my netbook and my entire firm comes with me. When I changed office locations, I did not need to transport boxes upon boxes of client files to the new building; I simply put my computer in a backpack. Coach Herman Boone from *Remember the Titans* might (accurately) describe my practice as "mobile, agile, hostile."

A paperless office also facilitates collaboration with clients, courts, co-counsel, and experts, as I will describe in greater detail in later sections of this chapter.

IV. HOW TO IMPLEMENT A PAPERLESS OFFICE

The following subsections describe in detail the tools I used to implement and maintain a paperless law office.

A. Scanner: Fujitsu ScanSnap s1500

A high-speed personal scanner is the backbone of a paperless law office, as this is the tool you will use to scan ***all*** incoming hard copies of documents.

As I discussed in Chapter 1, scanners that come attached to your printer are not suitable for use in a paperless office because they scan documents way too slowly, literally over 1,000 times slower than my scanner, the Fujitsu ScanSnap s1500. Accordingly, solos cannot afford to scrimp on their personal scanners. You can purchase the ScanSnap for about $400 on www.newegg.com, and I can assure you it is well worth the cost. Moreover, you will recoup the initial cost of the machine within months through savings on storage and printing costs.

It is critical that you place your ScanSnap on your desk so you can scan incoming hard copies contemporaneously with handling them. The ScanSnap is compact, so finding space should not be a problem. Before scanning, users should click on the ScanSnap icon that the ScanSnap software automatically adds to your desktop when you install the device. Under the "Scanning" tab, modify the ScanSnap's settings to automatically detect color and double-sided pages (note: the ScanSnap automatically detects different sizes of paper):

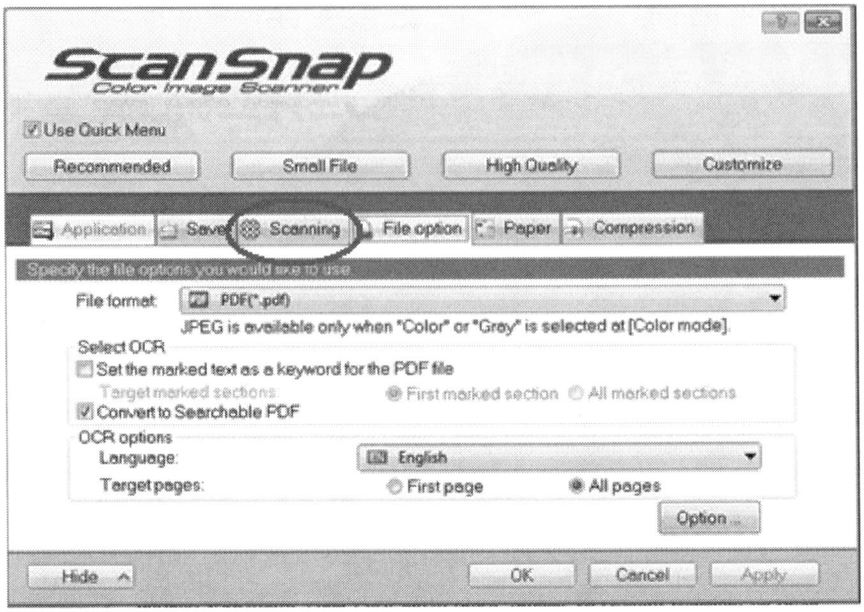

Under the "File option" tab, modify the ScanSnap's settings to automatically recognize text:

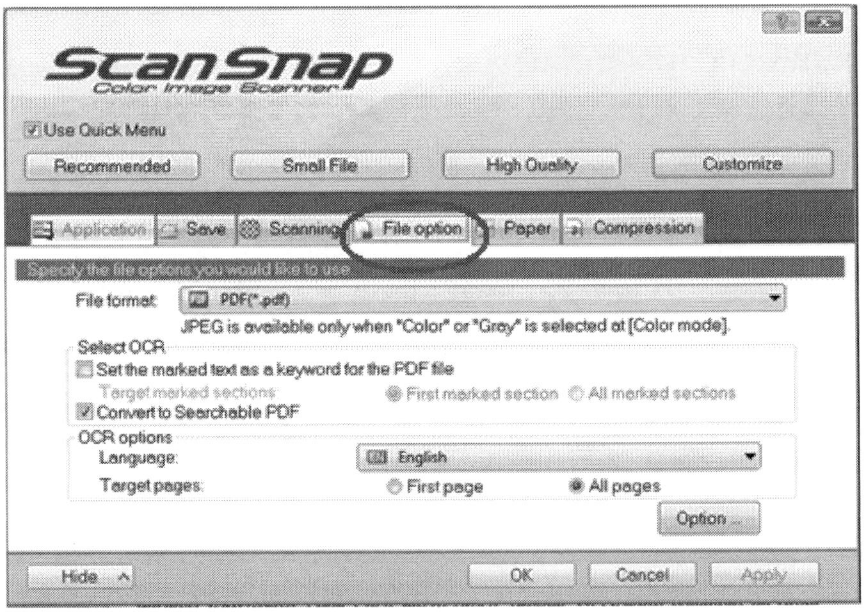

To scan documents you simply load the documents (up to 50 pages) into the automatic sheet feeder, press the scan button, and the ScanSnap starts scanning (I should note that I use the built-in scanner my all-in-one printer came equipped with to scan the occasional document the ScanSnap does not handle well). If the scan job exceeds 50 pages, simply add documents during the scan process. Visit http://vimeo.com/3890965, borrowed from the excellent legal blog, *Lawyerist* (available at www.lawyerist.com), to watch a video of the ScanSnap in action.

When the scan is complete, the ScanSnap will save the scanned documents as a single, searchable PDF file. In a later section of this chapter I will explain how and where to save the digital file on your computer's hard drive.

Finally, I cannot overemphasize the importance of scanning ***every*** hard copy you receive, as failure to do so defeats the objectives of a digital office.

B. <u>Adobe Acrobat Pro</u>

Adobe Acrobat Pro is the software you will use to manipulate, rather than merely view, the portable document format files (i.e., PDF files) that comprise the bulk of your paperless office. The ScanSnap comes bundled with Acrobat Standard, but I recommend that solos, particularly litigators, upgrade to Acrobat Pro because Acrobat Pro features redaction and Bates numbering tools, among other things. The following subsections highlight the features within Acrobat Pro I routinely use in my practice. I should note that Acrobat Standard has many of the same features as Acrobat Pro, but for organization and clarity I will refer to the software as "Acrobat Pro."

Visit http://tinyurl.com/2gxmz6r to upgrade to Acrobat Pro for about $200.

1. Edit PDFs

Most lawyers are familiar with the PDF file format yet perceive PDFs as mere static documents you view. Acrobat Pro enables users to add text, highlight, make notes, and otherwise manipulate a document however they want. In short, Acrobat Pro is Microsoft Word-lite combined with Paintbrush. Here is a screenshot of a PDF of this page I use to demonstrate a sampling of what Acrobat Pro can do:

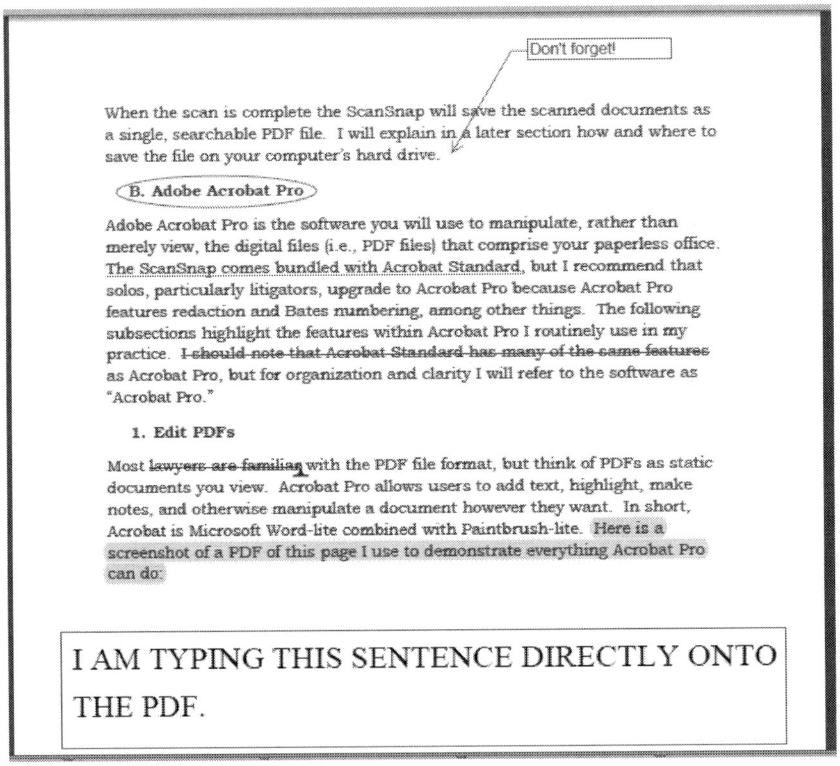

Don't forget!

When the scan is complete the ScanSnap will save the scanned documents as a single, searchable PDF file. I will explain in a later section how and where to save the file on your computer's hard drive.

B. Adobe Acrobat Pro

Adobe Acrobat Pro is the software you will use to manipulate, rather than merely view, the digital files (i.e., PDF files) that comprise your paperless office. The ScanSnap comes bundled with Acrobat Standard, but I recommend that solos, particularly litigators, upgrade to Acrobat Pro because Acrobat Pro features redaction and Bates numbering, among other things. The following subsections highlight the features within Acrobat Pro I routinely use in my practice. ~~I should note that Acrobat Standard has many of the same features~~ as Acrobat Pro, but for organization and clarity I will refer to the software as "Acrobat Pro."

1. Edit PDFs

Most ~~lawyers are familiar~~ with the PDF file format, but think of PDFs as static documents you view. Acrobat Pro allows users to add text, highlight, make notes, and otherwise manipulate a document however they want. In short, Acrobat is Microsoft Word-lite combined with Paintbrush-lite. Here is a screenshot of a PDF of this page I use to demonstrate everything Acrobat Pro can do:

I AM TYPING THIS SENTENCE DIRECTLY ONTO THE PDF.

The "typewriter" feature, which enables users to add text to PDFs, is the Acrobat Pro function I use most frequently. I frequently use other Acrobat Pro features such as the highlight tool or the callout dialog box on hard copies of documents I scan and convert to PDF files, such as opposing counsel's dispositive motion briefs, discovery materials, etc. I also like using Acrobat Pro's version of track changes when opposing counsel sends me a proposed settlement agreement in PDF format that contains terms I find objectionable.

2. Print as PDF

Acrobat Pro enables users to "print" e-mails, Word files, webpages, online articles or anything else users could otherwise print hard copies of via their printers. To clarify, Acrobat Pro enables users to convert the digital materials into PDF files and save the PDFs on your computer's hard drive. Simply open the dialog box to print how you normally would and select Adobe PDF as your printer:

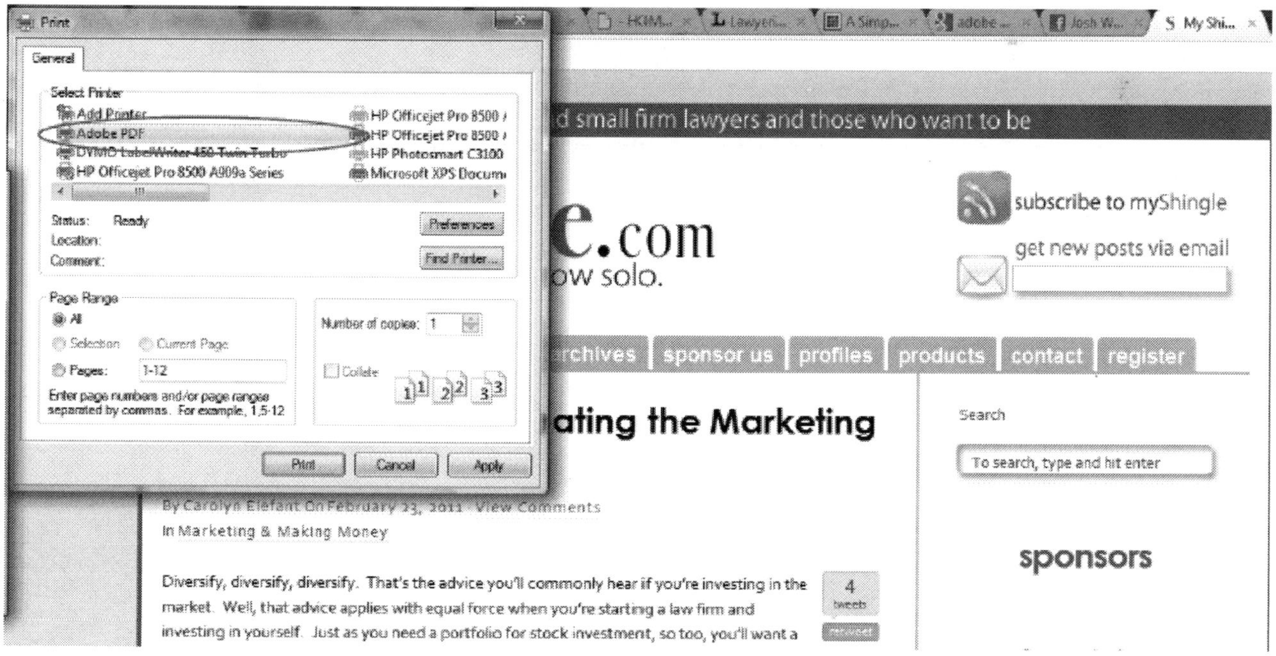

I use this function daily to "print" and save e-mails from clients and opposing counsel, caselaw, online articles, etc., as digital files.

3. Redactions and Bates numbering

Acrobat Pro has a powerful yet simple redaction feature that enables users to redact information one word or image at a time. Alternatively, users can use the search-and-redact feature by typing a word or phrase in a search box and Acrobat Pro searches the entire document and automatically redacts the word or phrase you typed:

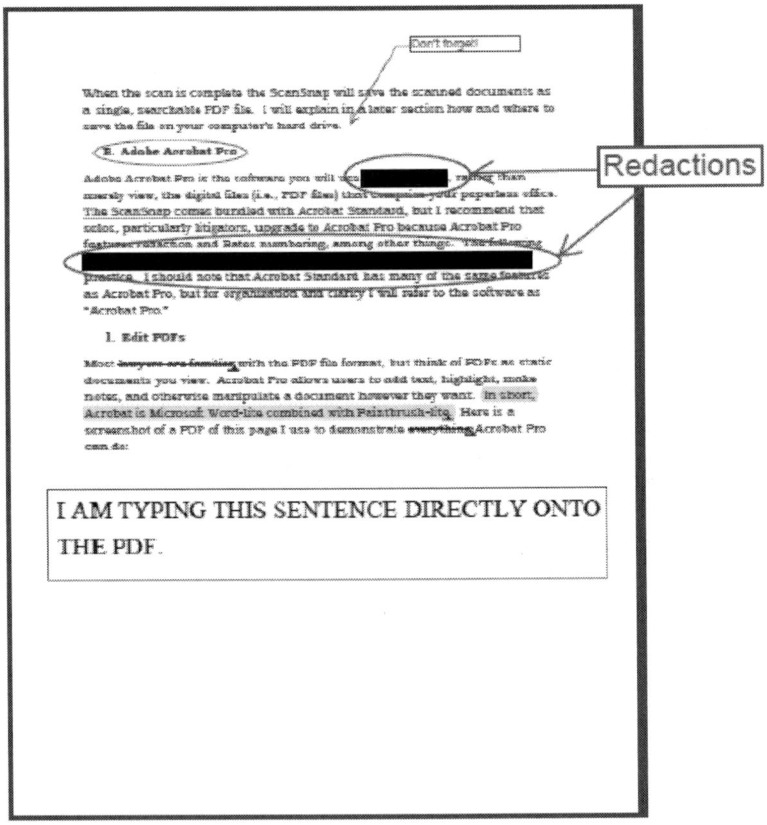

Acrobat Pro also enables users to add Bates numbering. As a litigator I use these features frequently in my practice.

4. Combine multiple PDFs into single PDF and delete pages

Acrobat Pro enables users to merge as many PDFs as they want into a single PDF:

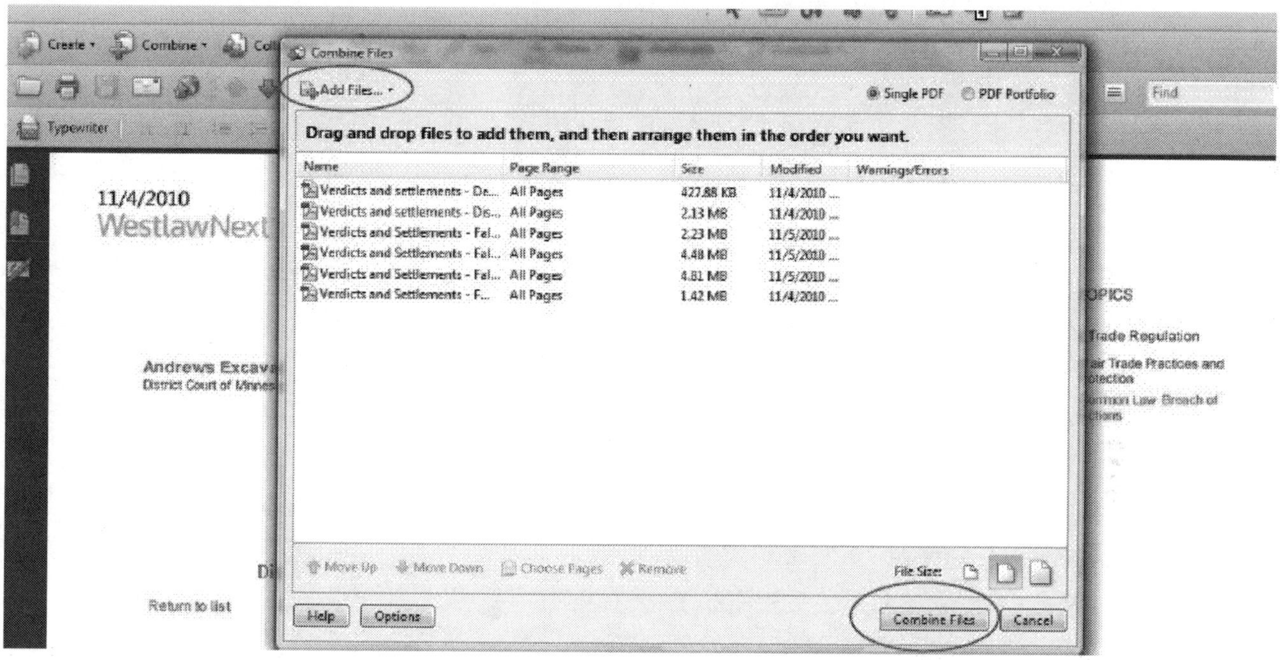

I use this feature frequently to respond to discovery requests and assemble exhibits. My only complaint is that Acrobat Pro does not allow users to merge non-PDF files into a single PDF file (i.e., you must first convert the document into PDF format), but I am picking nits here.

Acrobat Pro also enables users to delete pages within a PDF file.

5. Copy and paste text from PDFs into a Word file

Solos can use Acrobat Pro to copy text from a PDF file into a Word file:

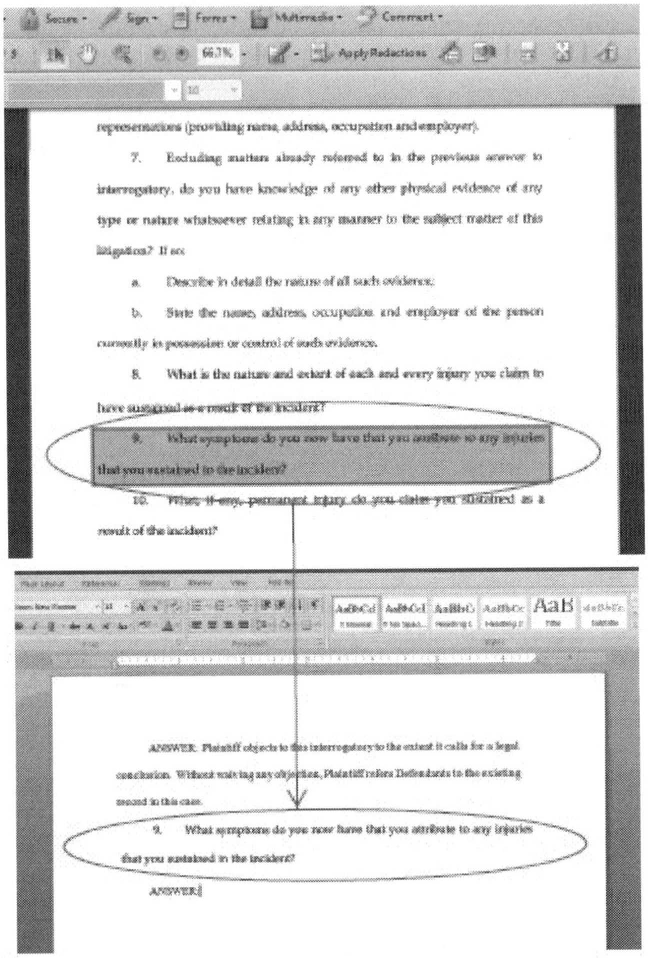

As a litigator I use this feature frequently when responding to discovery requests: instead of retyping individual requests, I simply copy and paste the request into the response I am drafting using Word, as illustrated in the graphic above.

C. Microsoft Office

Microsoft Office is a suite of programs that includes word processing, spreadsheet, database, and presentation software. Far and away, Office is the most popular office suite among lawyers and law firms. I do not recommend using free office suites such as Google Docs or OpenOffice.org because of performance and/or compatibility issues with Office. I do not recommend using the WordPerfect office suite (not free) for the same reasons. Most PCs come with a free 60-day trial version of Office. Visit http://tinyurl.com/48ouths to download the non-trial version for about $150.

The only Office program I use frequently in my practice is Word, the word processing program. Solos should take the time to learn Word because drafting documents is the heart of what most lawyers do. Word is a very powerful program, but most lawyers grossly underutilize its capabilities. Moreover, most lawyers just don't know how the program works—if you spend time grappling with numbering or formatting issues, that means you are ***not*** proficient in Word, and you should get formal training. At the very least, buy Office for Dummies on Amazon for $25.

For economic and efficiency reasons, solos ***must*** become self-reliant with respect to Word. If you pay an admin whose job duties mainly consist of composing or "cleaning up" your Word documents, you are wasting valuable resources. If your standard document drafting procedure consists of dictation, transcription, edit, enter corrections, edit, more corrections then you are engaging in the most inefficient means of drafting documents imaginable this side of ink and quill. If you graduated from law school and possess the chutzpah to start your own firm, I assure you that you can get proficient in Word.

A substantive discussion of Word features is beyond the scope of this book, but I will note that you should not transmit digital files to clients, opposing counsel, or courts unless you first convert the file into a PDF. This means you should not send "final drafts" of letters if the document is still in Word format. Not only does it look unprofessional, but you risk inadvertently disclosing confidential information through metadata (invisible data tracking the document's author, document changes, editing time, and other document properties) embedded in Word files. Accordingly, you should get familiar with converting Word documents into PDF files by using the "save as" function:

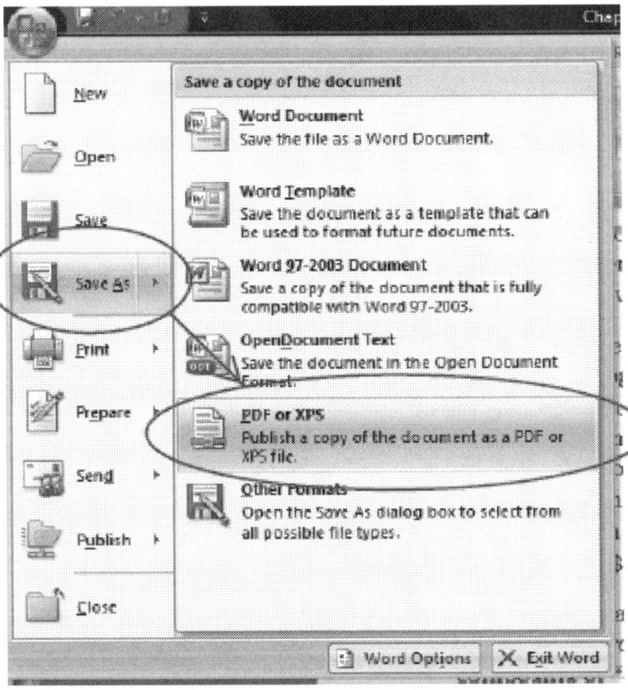

D. <u>Document Management System</u>

An effective, intuitive digital file naming and organization system is a necessary component of a digital law office.

As a solo you do not need to purchase fancy, expensive document management software. In fact, I believe such software impedes mobility and portability because it is tied to a hard drive or server.

I use a comprehensive file- and folder-naming system to manage my digital documents based on the system Donna Neff and Natalie Sanna discussed in their September 2009 *Law Practice Today* article, available at http://tinyurl.com/2e7jqer. I name all my documents in a consistent, uniform manner and save them within an intuitive, logical folder structure. My system requires strict adherence and consistent use and is therefore only suitable for solos who work with only one or two support staff members. If your team consists of more than three persons, I recommend you install "lockdown" document management software (e.g., Worldox at http://www.worldox.com) that prevents users from "going rogue" and circumventing the document management rules programmed into the software. I should also note that I am aware solos can use search software to locate documents stored on their hard drives, but I have found that relying exclusively on such software can result in wasted time.

In order to implement my system you must have a basic understanding of Windows Explorer folders. Visit http://tinyurl.com/4ub62s3 to learn how folders work.

The master parent folder for my system is named "My Dropbox" (I will discuss how Dropbox works in greater detail in a later section of this chapter). Nested under the master parent folder are my primary subfolders:

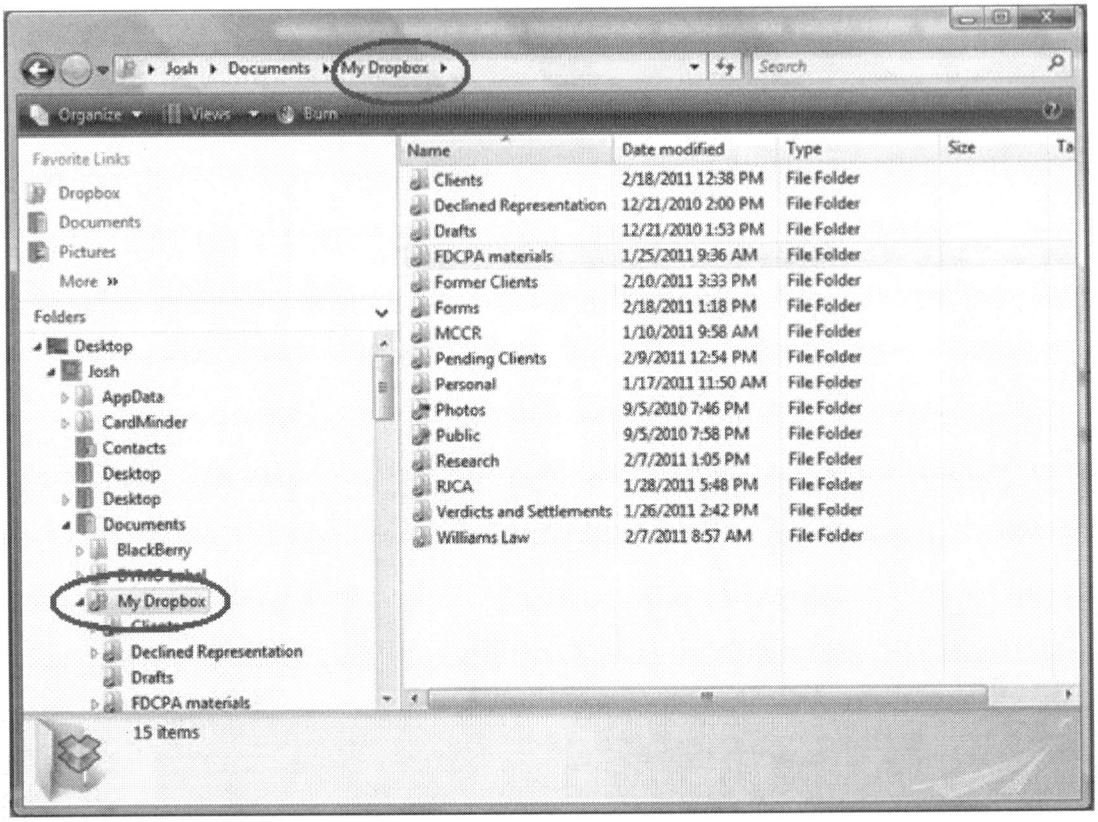

The following subsections discuss my most important primary subfolders.

1. Clients folder (and client document naming system)

This is the primary folder I use to store my active client files. I label each client folder as follows:

[Last Name], [First Name] – Matter Type

For example: "Doe, John – Employment"

Here are the subfolders I typically nest within each client folder:

The format for my client document naming system is as follows:

Client last name – Year.Month.Day – Concise description of document

For example: *Doe – 2011.02.23 – Defendant's memo in support of SJ*

Unlike the date listed in the Windows Explorer "Date Modified" column, the date following the client's name is static, thus Windows Explorer automatically sorts all documents within a folder chronologically. The date is when I created the document or received the document.

If I create a client document in Word or receive a client letter in Word format I will convert it to PDF format, name the document using the format outlined above, and store the document in the appropriate subfolder.

If I receive a hard copy of a client document (including executed retainer agreements) I will scan the hard copy into a PDF file, name the document using the format outlined above, and store the document in the appropriate subfolder.

If I "print" a client document (e.g., e-mails, caselaw, etc.) using Acrobat Pro I will name the document using the format outlined above and store the document in the appropriate subfolder.

If I receive a client document or a fax already in PDF format (e.g., letters from opposing counsel), I will rename the document using the format outlined above and store the document in the appropriate subfolder.

Finally, I follow the advice that Sam Glover, who uses a similar folder structure in his digital office, dispensed on his blog, *Lawyerist* (www.lawyerist.com):

> No Word, WordPerfect, Pages, OpenOffice.org, etc., file in any folders other than DRAFTS or NOTES & RESEARCH. Those files are not documents. They are drafts. PDFs or TIFFs are documents. Occasionally, if a client provides me a discoverable document in one of those formats, I will save it in that format in the /DOCS FROM CLIENT folder, since that digital file is the actual document they gave me.

2. Former Clients folder

This is the primary folder I use to store former client subfolders. Once I close a case, I simply move the client subfolder from the "Clients" primary folder to the "Former Clients" primary folder. I retain former client folders on my system because I frequently refer back to pleadings I drafted in old cases to use as templates in active cases, but if I ever get to the point where I am running low on storage space (I am not even close at present), I will transfer former client folders to an external hard drive.

3. Forms folder

This is the primary folder I use to store files I use as templates to create new documents. The files I store in this folder include all the different retainer agreements I use, pleadings for different types of cases, letterhead, etc. I must admit that the files stored in my Forms folder are arranged rather haphazardly, but creating appropriate subfolders is at the top of my to-do list.

4. Research folder

This is the primary folder I use to store research materials I locate in my cases. As I discussed in an earlier section of this chapter, I would often "reinvent the wheel" when I worked in Biglaw with respect to research in that I would perform redundant research on client files with similar issues. With a paperless office I can easily locate digital files of research materials I first identified in previous cases.

The way it works is that I created issue subfolders for all the issues that frequently come up in my cases:

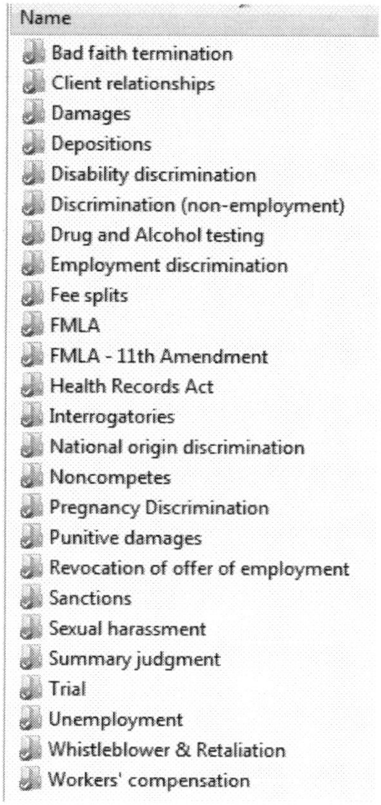

When I locate relevant caselaw, statutes, or articles in a case I am working on, I convert the materials into a PDF and save the digital file in both the "Research" subfolder nested under the client folder ***and*** under the applicable issue subfolder nested under the "Research" primary folder:

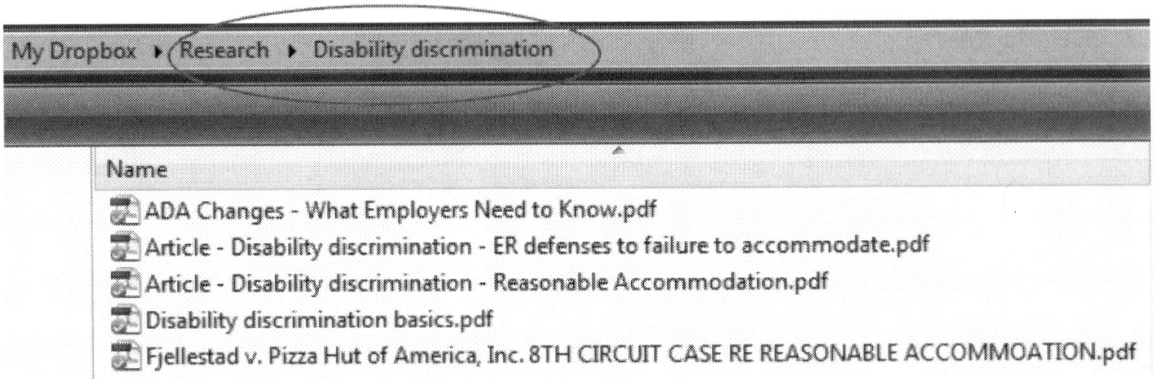

Thus, I can refer back to relevant research materials in seconds without having to recall the specific case I was working on when I first located the materials.

5. Verdicts and Settlements folder

This is the primary folder I use to store summaries of verdicts and settlements in the types of cases I litigate:

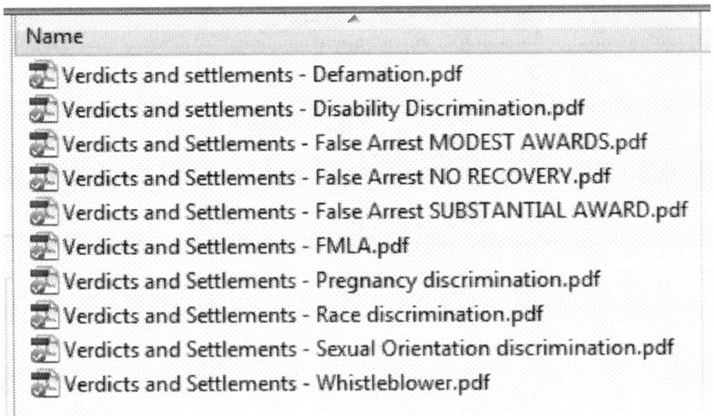

I use these documents to value cases and facilitate settlements.

6. Williams Law folder

This is the primary folder I use to store various files in my practice not tied to specific clients such as business plans, marketing ideas, articles I drafted, etc. I created subfolders for about a dozen categories, and each file is stored in a subfolder.

E. Google Quick Search Box

I can find most files instantly by strictly (slavishly?) adhering to the document management system outlined above. Every so often a document eludes me if I inadvertently misname the file or save it under the incorrect folder. In such situations I use the Google Quick Search Box to locate the "missing" file. Google Quick Search Box "floats" unobtrusively on your desktop:

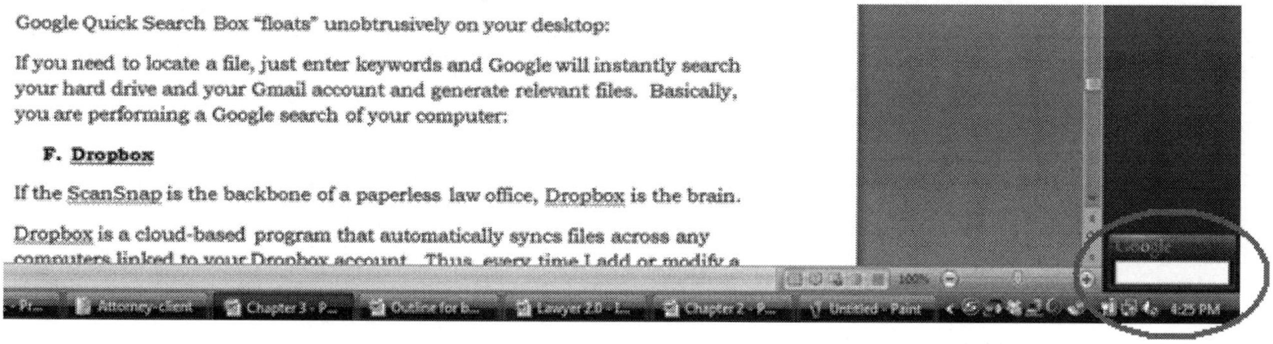

If you need to locate a file, just enter keywords and Google will instantly search your hard drive and your Gmail account and generate relevant files. Basically, you are performing a Google search of your computer:

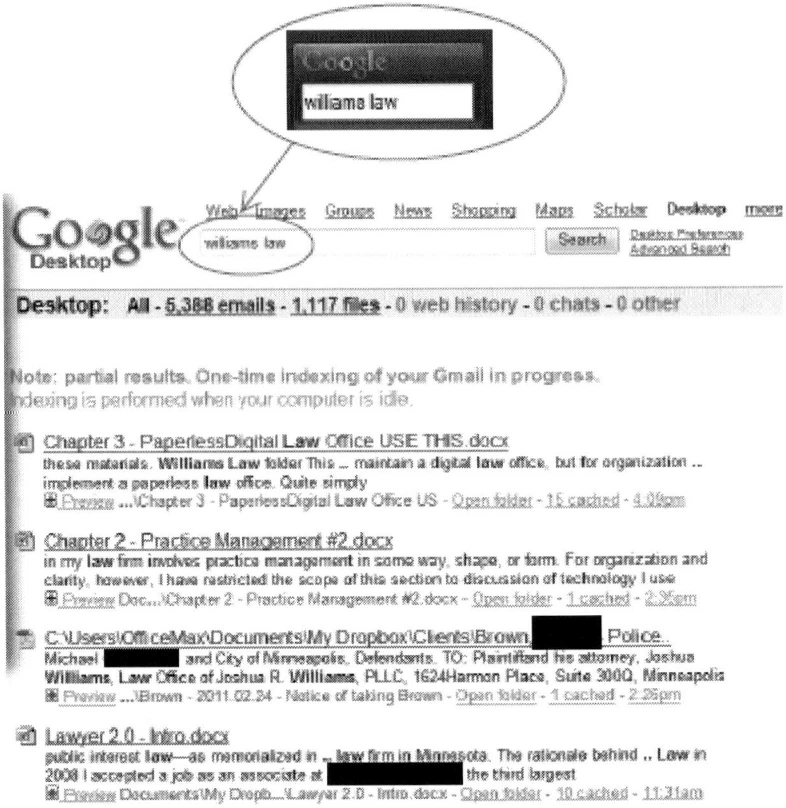

Please note that users can choose to view only files and exclude e-mails from search results, and vice-versa.

F. Dropbox

If the ScanSnap is the backbone of a paperless law office, Dropbox is the brain.

Dropbox is a Cloud-based program that automatically syncs files across any computers linked to your Dropbox account. Thus, every time I add or modify a file on my laptop, the addition or modification is automatically reflected on my netbook because both computers are linked to my Dropbox account. Dropbox also enables users to share individual folders with anyone else who has a Dropbox account. Thus, if I am working with co-counsel, experts, or my law clerk on a case I can grant them access to the particular client folder (i.e., rather than all my client folders) to facilitate collaboration. In this sense, I use Dropbox in my digital office much like a traditional law firm uses a server.

Dropbox works simply and elegantly. When you install Dropbox on your computer(s) it creates a "My Dropbox" folder nested under your Documents library on Windows Explorer:

As I discussed in an earlier section of this chapter, my Dropbox folder is the master parent folder that nests all the primary subfolders in my practice. When I add or modify a file saved in a folder nested under my Dropbox folder, Dropbox simultaneously saves the addition or modification to the Cloud and on any other computers with access to the folder where the file is stored.

Even if you lose internet connectivity you will still have access to your files nested under your Dropbox folder on your hard drive. If you add or modify a file when you lack internet connectivity, Dropbox will automatically sync the addition or modification with its website and any computers with access to the folder where the file is stored when you regain internet connectivity.

If you do not have access to your computer, you can access all your files from the Dropbox website via any device with internet connectivity, including your smartphone:

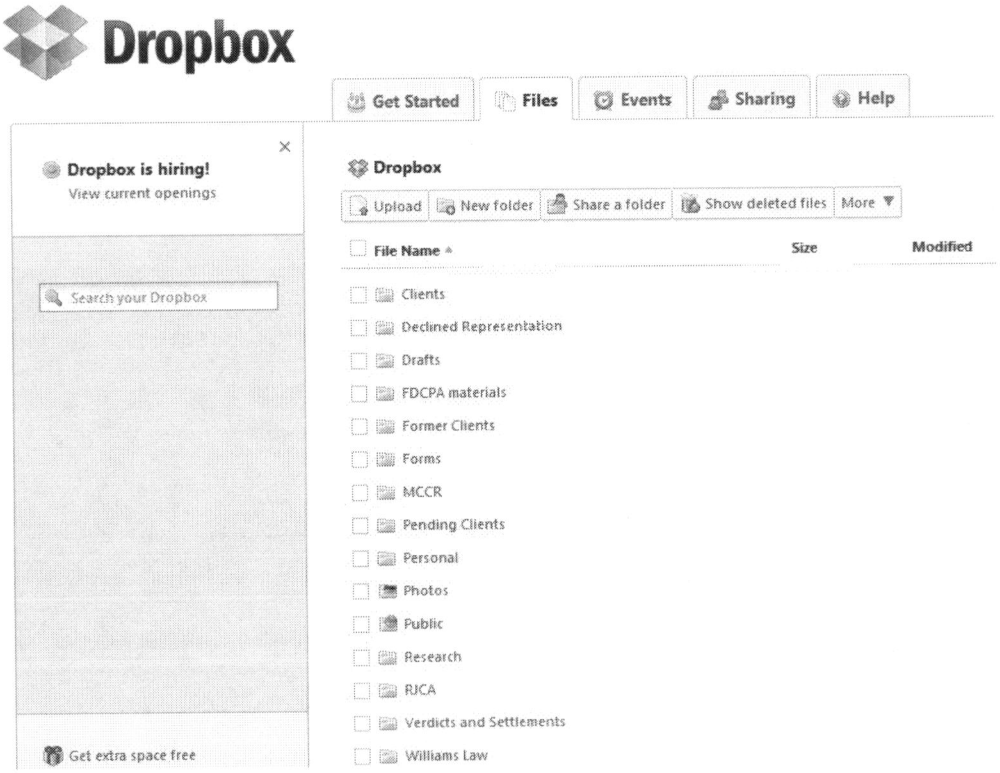

If both of my office computers crashed and I accidentally dropped my smartphone in the toilet on the same day, I could instantly regain every file in my practice by simply installing Dropbox on a replacement computer.

In summary, Dropbox provides solos with the mobility and portability they need to maximize the capabilities of their digital law offices.

Dropbox, available for download at www.dropbox.com, provides 2 GB of storage for free, 50 GB for $99 per year, and 100 GB for $199 per year. Solos can probably get by with the free subscription for the first year or two of solo practice.

G. **Backup**

It is critically important to back up all your digital files. As I discussed in Chapter 2, I put systems in place so my entire paperless office is automatically backed up in five different onsite and offsite locations.

H. **Shred Service**

I urge solos to refrain from keeping comprehensive parallel paper files of digital files because doing so is redundant and the paper file takes up precious space. I admit that when I work a case I typically maintain a small, physical "working file" that contains hard copies of certain documents I know I will want to refer to when drafting pleadings (e.g., notes from the initial client interview), but everything else gets shredded. I do not have the time or inclination to shred the documents myself, so I use a shred service. My shred service, First Shred, provides me with a lockable container that sits near my desk for easy access and serves double duty as my printer stand:

Shred Container

For $25 per month the shred man comes to my office once a month to empty my container, which is usually quite full by that point.

I. Gmail and Internet Fax Service

As I discussed in Chapter 2, I print hard copies of documents as seldom as possible. I send most documents out as attachments via e-mail, and for those who still insist on sending and receiving documents via fax I use the internet fax service I discussed in Chapter 2.

LAWYER 2.0 Legal Research

I. INTRODUCTION

As a litigator I perform a lot of legal research, and I perform almost all of my research online. I use area-specific print materials every so often (e.g., the ABA Employment Litigation Handbook and the NCLC Fair Debt Collection deskbook) to get the "30,000 foot view" of an issue, but given the narrow subject matter of this book I will limit the scope of this chapter to online legal research. The following subsections highlight the online legal research resources I frequently use in my practice.

II. GOOGLE SCHOLAR

Many of the partners at the Biglaw firm where I used to work would routinely ration my Westlaw use when they assigned research projects. The partners' stated rationale for imposing Westlaw restrictions was to reduce client costs (like most large firms, my firm passed Westlaw costs on to its clients), and I conducted most of my research the old-fashioned way in the firm library.

It does not take an NBA salary cap expert to figure out that the partners' calculus was fundamentally flawed. To clarify, caselaw that would take me ten minutes to locate on Westlaw via a $50 database search would take me two hours to locate "the old-fashioned way," and my hourly billing rate was [way more than $50]. Regardless of the partners' rationale, I found Westlaw restrictions to be quite challenging because I had grown accustomed in law school to using my free Westlaw student account to run up scores of meandering caselaw searches with impunity.

Now that I am a solo who works cases under contingency fee arrangements and does not pass Westlaw costs on to clients, I have legitimate reasons to minimize research costs. Fortunately, Google Scholar is a great tool for conducting the caselaw "fishing expeditions" I carried out via Westlaw back in law school.

Google Scholar, available at scholar.google.com, is a free online program that enables users to perform Google searches on federal and state caselaw. Google Scholar's database contains all recent published opinions, as well as some unpublished opinions. Google Scholar enables users to narrow the scope of their searches to specific courts, and displays the full text of the opinion with accurate pagination and hyperlinks to internal citations:

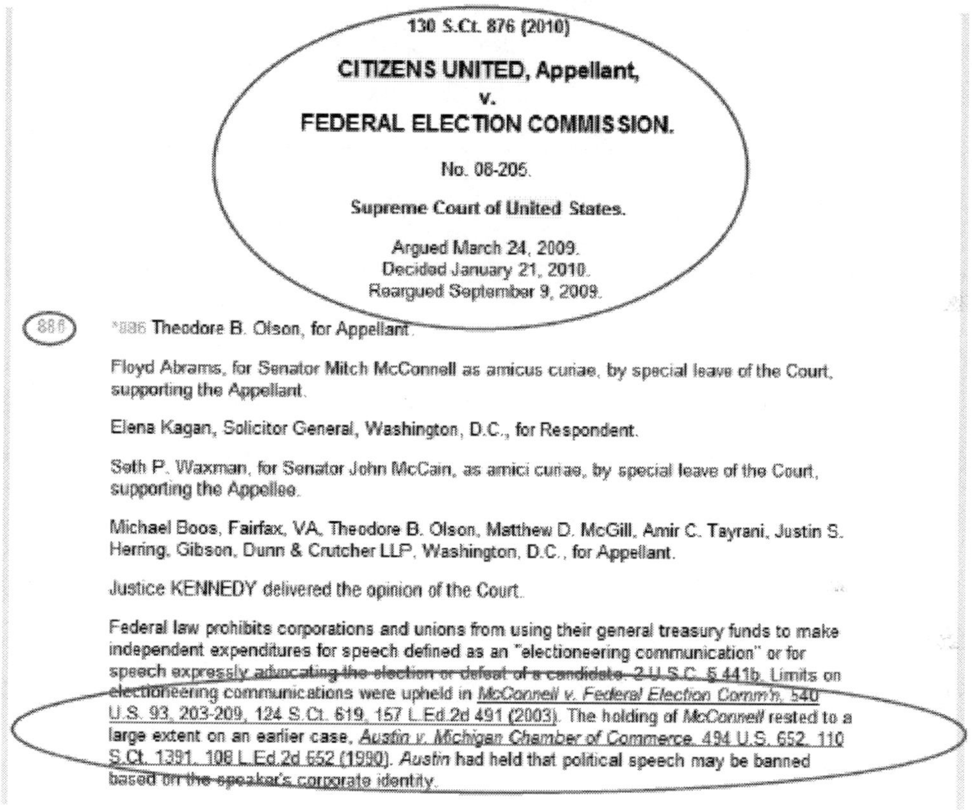

130 S.Ct. 876 (2010)

CITIZENS UNITED, Appellant,
v.
FEDERAL ELECTION COMMISSION.

No. 08-205.

Supreme Court of United States.

Argued March 24, 2009.
Decided January 21, 2010.
Reargued September 9, 2009.

886

*886 Theodore B. Olson, for Appellant.

Floyd Abrams, for Senator Mitch McConnell as amicus curiae, by special leave of the Court, supporting the Appellant.

Elena Kagan, Solicitor General, Washington, D.C., for Respondent.

Seth P. Waxman, for Senator John McCain, as amici curiae, by special leave of the Court, supporting the Appellee.

Michael Boos, Fairfax, VA, Theodore B. Olson, Matthew D. McGill, Amir C. Tayrani, Justin S. Herring, Gibson, Dunn & Crutcher LLP, Washington, D.C., for Appellant.

Justice KENNEDY delivered the opinion of the Court.

Federal law prohibits corporations and unions from using their general treasury funds to make independent expenditures for speech defined as an "electioneering communication" or for speech expressly advocating the election or defeat of a candidate. 2 U.S.C. § 441b. Limits on electioneering communications were upheld in *McConnell v. Federal Election Comm'n,* 540 U.S. 93, 203-209, 124 S.Ct. 619, 157 L.Ed.2d 491 (2003). The holding of *McConnell* rested to a large extent on an earlier case, *Austin v. Michigan Chamber of Commerce,* 494 U.S. 652, 110 S.Ct. 1391, 108 L.Ed.2d 652 (1990). *Austin* had held that political speech may be banned based on the speaker's corporate identity.

When I locate a relevant case I "print" the case as a PDF file and store the file in the research folder nested under my client folder. I then use Acrobat Pro to mark the case up as I see fit:

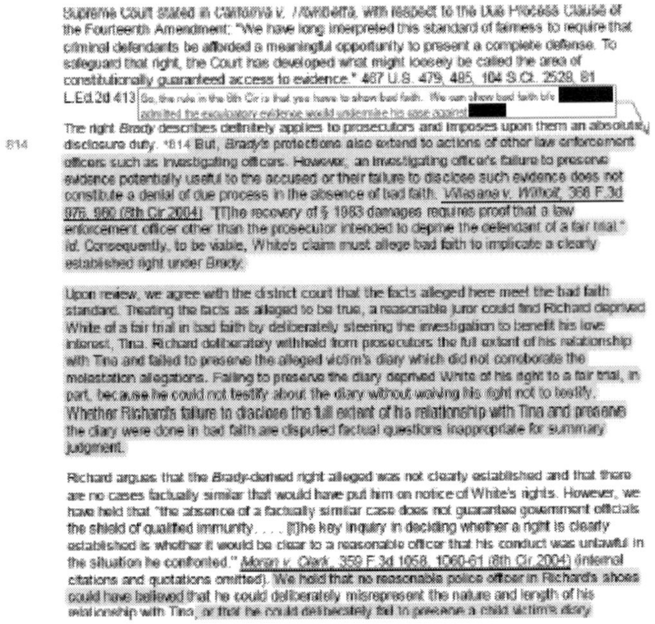

Supreme Court stated in California v. Trombetta, with respect to the Due Process Clause of the Fourteenth Amendment: "We have long interpreted this standard of fairness to require that criminal defendants be afforded a meaningful opportunity to present a complete defense. To safeguard that right, the Court has developed what might loosely be called the area of constitutionally guaranteed access to evidence." 467 U.S. 479, 485, 104 S.Ct. 2528, 81 L.Ed.2d 413

So, the rule in the 8th Cir is that you have to show bad faith. We can show bad faith b/c [redacted] admitted the exculpatory evidence would undermine his case against [redacted]

The right Brady describes definitely applies to prosecutors and imposes upon them an absolute disclosure duty.
814 *814 But, Brady's protections also extend to actions of other law enforcement officers such as investigating officers. However, an investigating officer's failure to preserve evidence potentially useful to the accused or their failure to disclose such evidence does not constitute a denial of due process in the absence of bad faith. Villasana v. Wilhoit, 368 F.3d 976, 980 (8th Cir.2004). "[T]he recovery of § 1983 damages requires proof that a law enforcement officer other than the prosecutor intended to deprive the defendant of a fair trial." Id. Consequently, to be viable, White's claim must allege bad faith to implicate a clearly established right under Brady.

Upon review, we agree with the district court that the facts alleged here meet the bad faith standard. Treating the facts as alleged to be true, a reasonable juror could find Richard deprived White of a fair trial in bad faith by deliberately steering the investigation to benefit his love interest, Tina. Richard deliberately withheld from prosecutors the full extent of his relationship with Tina and failed to preserve the alleged victim's diary which did not corroborate the molestation allegations. Failing to preserve the diary deprived White of his right to a fair trial, in part, because he could not testify about the diary without waiving his right not to testify. Whether Richard's failure to disclose the full extent of his relationship with Tina and preserve the diary were done in bad faith are disputed factual questions inappropriate for summary judgment.

Richard argues that the Brady-derived right alleged was not clearly established and that there are no cases factually similar that would have put him on notice of White's rights. However, we have held that "the absence of a factually similar case does not guarantee government officials the shield of qualified immunity. . . . [T]he key inquiry in deciding whether a right is clearly established is whether it would be clear to a reasonable officer that his conduct was unlawful in the situation he confronted." Moran v. Clark, 359 F.3d 1058, 1060-61 (8th Cir.2004) (internal citations and quotations omitted). We hold that no reasonable police officer in Richard's shoes could have believed that he could deliberately misrepresent the nature and length of his relationship with Tina, or that he could deliberately fail to preserve a child victim's diary

The primary weaknesses of Google Scholar are (1) lack of a true Shepardizing tool, (2) no links to primary law, and (3) a database that goes back only 50 years for federal caselaw and 80 years for state caselaw and does not include all unpublished cases.

With respect to the first weakness, a simple workaround is to sort the case results by date, and if the case in question has been overruled, the newest cases will reflect that fact. If the newest cases still rely on that ruling, odds are the case in question is still good law. If the case is a crucially important case that you want to hang your hat on, then you should perform an a la carte Shepardize search on Lexis (http://law.lexisnexis.com/shepards) or Keycite search on Westlaw (http://tinyurl.com/4hrqkf7).

With respect to the second weakness, you can simply copy and paste citations into Google and locate the full text of the statute, rule, or regulation.

With respect to the third weakness, you probably shouldn't be relying on authority over 50 years old or unpublished cases anyway.

III. PREMIUM ONLINE RESEARCH SERVICE

I highly recommend that litigators subscribe to a premium online research service (i.e., Westlaw or Lexis). Google Scholar is great for caselaw searches, but I believe solo litigators need access to more resources in order to keep pace with the large firms they are often adverse to.

Until recently the Westlaw or Lexis choice was simply a matter of which interface users felt comfortable with. In my case, the firm where I worked at before going solo used Westlaw, so I decided to subscribe to Westlaw.

In Fall 2010, however, Lexis launched a product aimed squarely at solos called Lexis Advance (available at http://www.lexisnexis.com/NewLexis/Advance) that changes the complexion of the premium legal research service for solos landscape. With the introduction of Lexis Advance I believe solos' practice areas and jurisdictions, rather than interface preferences, should dictate which service they choose.

WestlawNext (available at http://tinyurl.com/274v7yd) and Lexis Advance are "Web 2.0" products from Westlaw and Lexis, respectively. Both have a Google-esque look and feel: a simple, clean interface with one search box where users type in natural search terms "Google-style," and an advanced search option where you can run Boolean searches:

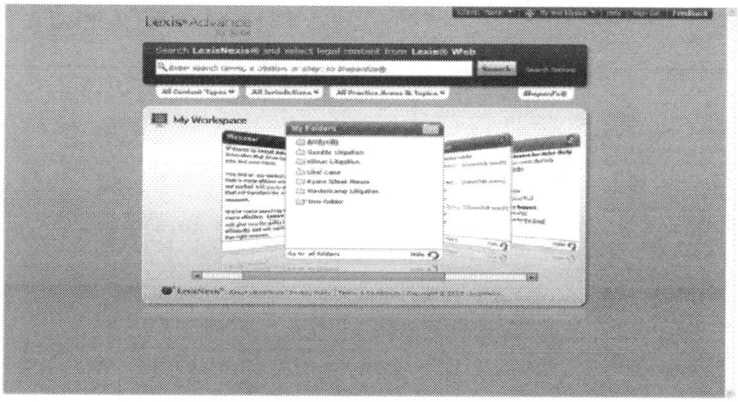

Lexis Advance

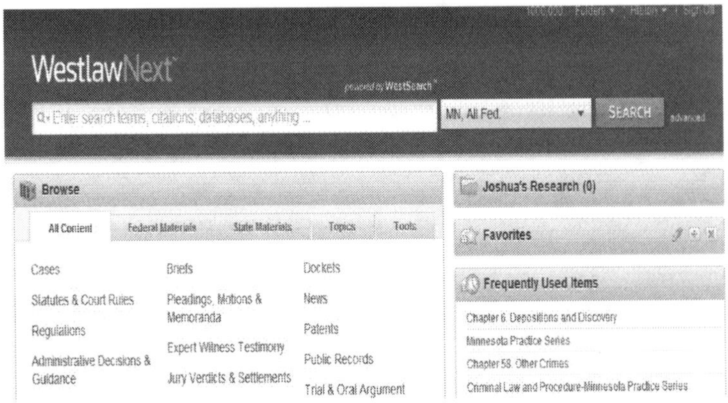

WestlawNext

WestlawNext and Lexis Advance are way easier to use than their predecessor versions, and if you are still using an older version there is not a good reason to refrain from upgrading because the cost is roughly the same.

I believe Lexis Advance represents the best value for most solos. For a $175 monthly flat fee ($315 for two attorneys) users get unlimited access to all case and statutory law from all state and federal jurisdictions; Shepard's Citations; jury verdicts, briefs, pleadings, and motions, including premium materials from IDEX; CourtLink content with the full collection of dockets; and expert witness transcripts, depositions, and curricula vitae. Users also get unlimited access to 24 different treatises and forms databases. Visit http://tinyurl.com/6fa2kq5 for a full list of databases that come with Lexis Advance.

The only drawback to Lexis Advance is that the product does not allow users to access content outside of the materials set forth above. A "closed" subscription should not be a problem for most users because Lexis Advance comes with so much content.

Unless it is.

I pay about $250 per month for my WestlawNext subscription, yet I have access to way less content than Lexis Advance offers. My subscription does not include access to caselaw or primary law; rather, my subscription "plan" is a hodgepodge of databases I have unlimited access to that I selected based on my practice areas. I should note that I had to haggle with my Westlaw rep to get the price point down to about $250 per month.

I am locked into multiyear indentured servitude to WestlawNext, so switching to Lexis Advance is a non-option for me. Even if switching was an option, I would still stick with WestlawNext because the online treatises I use most frequently—Minnesota Practice Series (which is basically a state-specific AmJur), a few employment litigation treatises, and Wright & Miller *Practice and Procedure*—do not come with the Lexis Advance subscription (I should note that Lexis Advance comes with *Moore's Federal Practice*, but I prefer Wright & Miller).

In summary, WestlawNext is ideal for me, especially since Google Scholar obviates the need for caselaw access in a premium legal research service: if a WestlawNext treatise links to a case I simply copy and paste the citation into Google Scholar to get the full text of the case. For solos who do not practice in Minnesota and whose primary practice area is not employment litigation, Lexis Advance is probably your best option.

IV. ONLINE TREATISES

I was performing a keyword search on Google concerning an employment law issue and the search results generated a page from an excellent online employment discrimination treatise, *Garland's Digest* (available at http://www.garlands-digest.com). *Garland's Digest* is the only free online treatise I have encountered that is helpful to my practice, but I imagine there are other free resources in different areas of the law that are useful.

V. ONLINE PRIMARY LAW

The State of Minnesota publishes a website, available at https://www.revisor.mn.gov/statutes, that contains a database of all applicable state statutes, session laws, rules and court rules. I believe most states maintain similarly-comprehensive websites. I do not use the Minnesota website frequently because the treatises included in my WestlawNext subscription contain comprehensive information on the primary laws that are at-issue in my practice areas, but every now and then the website comes in handy (e.g., in whistleblower cases where I need to perform research on the underlying law(s) my clients claim their employers terminated them for reporting violations of).

Additionally, the Office of the Federal Register maintains an online database, available at http://tinyurl.com/ye6rpl6, of the Code of Federal Regulations that I frequently refer to.

I should note that if you subscribe to Lexis Advance, you already have access to annotated versions of all federal and state primary law.

VI. SECRETARY OF STATE WEBSITES

I frequently sue large, out-of-state or multinational organizations operating under assumed names, thus I need to determine the appropriate name of the putative defendant and where to effectuate service of process. The Minnesota Secretary of State maintains a website where users can obtain this information for free. I believe most states' secretary of state offices maintain similar websites.

VII. ONLINE CASE RECORDS

The State of Minnesota Judicial Branch maintains a website that contains a database of trial court records of all adjudicated criminal and civil matters. I use this database to run the names of individual defendants in my cases to see if they have criminal records (and to check the criminal records of my clients to determine if they are sympathetic plaintiffs).

VIII. GOOGLE

Google has become such a ubiquitous presence in our online lives that we sometimes take it for granted, but do not forget that Google can be a powerful weapon in your online research arsenal. With this in mind, I perform Google searches at the beginning of every research project where the issue is completely foreign to me to get the "30,000 foot view," and at the end of any research project to see if there are any materials out there that I missed.

I also use Google to locate sample pleadings in cases where I have not already developed a template.

LAWYER 2.0 Online Marketing

I. INTRODUCTION

It may sound crass to some lawyers, but for solos good lawyering is a secondary consideration to good marketing. Quite literally, we cannot practice law unless we *have* a practice.

There is a lot that goes into good legal marketing, including networking, teaching CLEs, writing articles, taking pro bono cases, joining volunteer boards, getting good press, print advertising, television advertising, and other strategies. Given the narrow focus of this book, I have limited the scope of this chapter to online marketing techniques, and I highly recommend that you visit the following blogs to learn more about traditional marketing techniques: *Legal Practice Pro* (www.legalpracticepro.com), *Lawyerist* (www.lawyerist.com), *MyShingle* (www.myshingle.com), the *Attorney Marketing Blog* (http://tinyurl.com/cq3ehh), and even *Above The Law* (www.abovethelaw.com). I should note that I frequently read these materials to learn more about online and traditional marketing strategies.

When I launched my firm in Minneapolis in Fall 2009 I had only been admitted to practice for less than one year, I had only lived in the area since July 2008, and I did not attend law school at one of the four area law schools. In short, I had zero connections or potential referral sources, and I calculated that online marketing would give me the best shot at getting my name out to prospective clients.

Accordingly, I focused nearly all of my marketing resources towards online marketing, and I built a six-figure practice in less than 12 months.

The following sections highlight the online marketing strategies I use in my practice.

II. WEBSITE

Solos need a clean, professional-looking website. If you do not have a website or your website looks unprofessional, it signals to colleagues, clients, courts, and opposing counsel that your firm is a small-time operation without any infrastructure. I believe a strong online presence is so critical to your firm's success that you should refrain from launching your solo practice until you have a professional-looking website up and running. If you launch prematurely, you risk being labeled as a hack.

I should note that having a professional-looking website is not as important for solos who have been in business for years and have a strong referral network in place. For everyone else, you need a good-looking website.

The following subsections describe considerations that should go into building your firm's website.

A. Domain Name

Your domain name is your web address and designates your firm (e.g., www.jrwilliamslaw.com) or your practice area (e.g., www.mnemploymentattorney.com). I recommend registering both a descriptive domain name and a domain that designates your firm name and designing your website so that it automatically redirects visitors from one site to the other. You can register domain names relatively cheaply (less than $10 per year) at several registration sites, including www.godaddy.com, www.inmotionhosting.com, etc.

Please note that you should avoid using the name of the host server in your web address (e.g., www.wordpress.jrwilliamslaw.com) because it looks unprofessional.

B. Content

First and foremost, your website should communicate to prospective clients what you can do for them, as opposed to merely touting your own accomplishments. You should still communicate your accomplishments and competence, but frame them in such a manner that the aim is to demonstrate to the prospective client how they may benefit the client. Download Tom O'Leary's free e-book (available at http://www.the-attorneys-atm.com/register-here.html) and refer to Chapter 9 for strategies on how to accomplish this objective.

You should also use plain English rather than legalese to avoid coming across as pompous. That said, you should refrain from talking down to your target audience to avoid coming across as patronizing. Even if you are running a consumer firm, a potential client who is savvy enough to locate you via the internet is going to appreciate a lawyer with a sincere, straightforward, serious message, rather than fluff touting your "toughness" and "aggressiveness."

At a minimum, your website should include the following pages: (1) Home page, (2) Bio, (3) FAQ, (4) Contact, and (5) pages for each area of practice. Take a look at my firm's website at www.jrwilliamslaw.com for ideas on how to craft the content on your website.

C. Cost, Web Hosting, and Design

There are plenty of web hosting companies that offer free or very inexpensive (i.e., under $300) do-it-yourself website packages, but such services tend to place third-party forced ads on your site, which you should avoid because they make your site look unprofessional.

Some web hosting companies offer create-your-own website packages without forced ads and claim that subscribers who lack technological know-how can build their own websites. If you have never built a website, your firm website should not be your first cyber-canvas. Solos who lack website building experience should contact a professional web developer who can build a website with modest customization for under $1,000. I recommend my website developer, Eben Laurie (www.optimizeguys.com), who can work with solos from anywhere in the country. If you prefer to work with a local web designer, I suggest you identify local firms with websites you like and ask the attorney(s) to provide you with the web designer's name and contact information.

I do not recommend hiring Findlaw to build your website. Findlaw will build you a website that looks good and is well-optimized (I will discuss optimization in greater detail later in this chapter). Unfortunately, Findlaw builds "cookie-cutter" websites, so you run the risk of having the look and feel of your site being strikingly similar to your competitors' websites. Additionally, Findlaw reps may use a "hard-sell" sales approach—my putative rep all but told me that I was not a real lawyer unless I hired Findlaw to build my website—that I believe is aimed at preying on solos' insecurity. Finally, I do not believe the Findlaw product is worth the cost, which the rep quoted at around $500 per month.

The less customization your website has, the less it will cost. Customized features that can drive up cost include animated graphics, large graphics, and embedded videos. I purposely avoided these features on my website because they tend to take a long time to load and I knew many members of my target audience were lower-income folk who used older, slower computers or had slow-speed internet connections; I just wanted a clean-looking site without the bells and whistles. If slow loading speed is not likely to be an issue for your target audience, then you may want to consider increased customization. Take a look at your competitors' websites to determine what customized features your target audience will expect.

Solos should definitely include an updated, professional photo on their homepages and bio pages. I was reluctant to put my photo on the homepage because I thought it might look undignified, but the fact that several clients have told me that seeing my photo made them feel more comfortable calling me validates my decision.

Finally, many reputable companies offer web hosting (i.e., providing space on a server to host your site) for under $100 per year. I pay InMotion Hosting (www.inmotionhosting.com) about eight dollars per month to host three websites and have no complaints. If your website developer insists on hosting your website and charging you more than $10 per month, you may want to ask him or her to use another hosting service. Some solos who already have websites pay hundreds of dollars each month for web hosting. If this describes you I strongly suggest you contact Tom O'Leary (www.the-attorneys-atm.com) to discuss moving your site to a less expensive web hosting provider.

D. Wordpress

I highly recommend that solos build their websites using the Wordpress platform, available at www.wordpress.com.

Wordpress started in 2003 as open-source web software that enabled users to publish their own blogs, but developers have since added features that enable web designers to build entire websites on the Wordpress platform.

Wordpress features a user-friendly interface and preloaded themes that enable users without any technological knowledge to start a blog in minutes. In order to create a Wordpress website with a professional look and feel, you need some web design experience. That said, Wordpress is still easy enough to use that creating new pages and adding and editing content require no programming experience.

Once a web designer sets up the "bones" of your site, you can manage content and make site updates on your own rather than wait days or weeks for your web developer. I mentioned in Chapter 3 that I believe self-reliance with respect to Microsoft Word is essential for solos. In order for solos to maximize their practices, this self-reliance must extend to all areas of their practices.

Finally, I should note that my firm's website is not built on the Wordpress platform, but only because I stupidly failed to take my web developer's advice. Your web developer might charge you more to build a Wordpress site because she knows she will lose future fees given that you will not need to hire her to add new content to your site, but I can assure you a Wordpress site will pay for itself over time: the cost of the website updates I made over the past year exceeds the difference between the initial cost of my website and what my web developer would have charged me to build a Wordpress site.

III. SEARCH ENGINE OPTIMIZATION (SEO)

When you type a query in search engines' search box, search engines generate two types of results: organic (unpaid) and inorganic (paid):

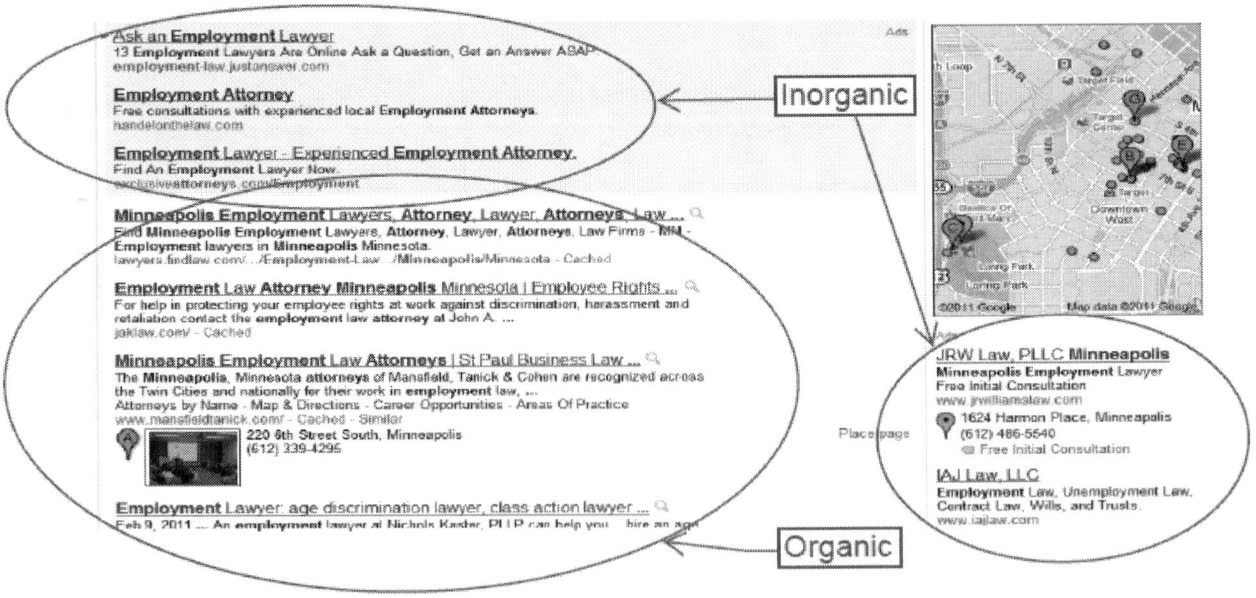

SEO is the process of improving the visibility of a website's organic search listing.

Web developers often claim that they will build you an "optimized" website, but in reality your site may not give the search engines what they want to see. Accordingly, solos may need to hire an SEO consultant in order to rank highly on search engines.

SEO may not be critically important for solos whose target audience includes sophisticated business entities or high-income individuals because these potential clients rely on referral networks rather than the internet and advertisements to locate attorneys. That said, solos with such a target audience still need a professional-looking website because their potential clients expect them to have a strong online presence.

SEO *is* critically important for solos whose target audience includes people who don't know lawyers. Potential clients who know a lawyer will contact that lawyer when they have a legal issue, even if the issue is beyond the scope of the lawyer's expertise, because they know the lawyer can refer them to someone who can help (for this reason alone it is essential for solos to build referral networks, but traditional marketing is beyond the scope of this book). Most potential clients who do not know a lawyer will look to the internet when they need legal assistance.

As little as ten years ago such persons would look in the yellow pages to find lawyers, but now that two-thirds of American adults have high-speed internet access at home (and many of the remaining third have internet access at work or via their mobile phones), according to the Pew Research Center, most now use the internet. Some solos still spend thousands of dollars each year on yellow pages ads, which I believe amounts to throwing your money down the toilet (unless your target audience was born prior to the Eisenhower Administration). It is counter-intuitive to presume that your potential clients would use the yellow pages to locate a service provider given that it has probably been years since you did the same.

I concede you can still potentially capture the roughly 20 percent of Americans who lack internet access by running a yellow pages ad, but in most cases the high cost does not justify the return on investment. If you still own a yellow pages phone book, you can turn to the "attorneys" section and find pages and pages of ads (32 pages in the Minneapolis yellow pages). Thus, most attorney ads are going to get lost in the shuffle. If you have the resources to purchase a full-page color ad or you are advertising a unique practice area, purchasing a yellow pages ad might make sense. Every other solo, however, should spend her advertising dollars on SEO.

Everything I know about SEO I learned from Tom O'Leary, an SEO consultant who works almost exclusively with lawyers. I followed the free advice he dispenses on his blog, website, and e-book, and in less than one month my website was ranked on the first page of Google for my relevant search terms. I did it all on my own and without spending any money.

Rather than regurgitate O'Leary's content, I will simply direct you to visit his website at www.the-attorneys-atm.com.

Some of O'Leary's strategies are easy to implement, while others require some tech savvy. I suggest you implement everything your skill level permits, wait about a month (SEO strategies can take some time to marinate), and see what results you get. If you practice in a small or rural community, you can get page one rankings relatively easily. If you practice in a populous market in a competitive area of law, you may need to hire O'Leary to implement the strategies that require some expertise.

Once my website achieved page one rankings my practice took off and generated enough fees to justify spending money on some of the paid SEO strategies O'Leary suggests (I also hired Tom to make a few tweaks to my overall SEO strategy). These days my website ranks in the top five results on page one of Google for all of my relevant search terms.

Finally, I must clarify that Mr. O'Leary has not paid me a cent to promote his work. Rather, I am merely grateful to him for providing me with some of the most important tools I needed to build a six-figure practice in less than 12 months.

IV. ONLINE LEGAL DIRECTORIES

Creating listings for your firm on online legal directories is really just one component of SEO, but it is important enough that it merits its own section.

There are dozens of free and paid online legal directories. In most cases prospective clients will not find you via the online directory, but because of the way search engines work (the more websites that point to your website, the more important your website becomes in the eyes of search engines), creating an online listing will drive traffic to your website. Listings on the paid directories Lexis and Westlaw operate are very expensive, and new solos who lack the resources should not feel compelled to create listings. Listings offered by state and local bar associations and practice group associations tend to be relatively inexpensive (i.e., less than $100 per year), and I highly recommend that solos invest in creating such listings if they allow you to link to your website.

V. ONLINE REFERRAL SERVICES

Online referral services work by harvesting potential clients and referring them to lawyers for a fee. I shied away from referral services because they tend to be expensive—up to $4,000 per year—and their business models did not jive with me philosophically.

I know several lawyers who signed up for online referral services, and none of them were impressed with the product.

VI. ONLINE ADVERTISEMENTS IN LEGAL PUBLICATIONS

If you are just starting out, I suggest you consider placing an ad on your local bar association's website advertising your availability to perform contract work. I used this strategy to secure *of counsel* contract work within a few weeks after I went solo, which generated income while I nurtured my fledging contingency fee practice.

VII. BLOGGING

Some lawyers claim that blogging is the most important online marketing tool in their practices, arguing that they attract new business by demonstrating their expertise in an area of law via their blog. Given recent changes Google made to its algorithm, however, I do not believe blogging is likely to generate enough business to justify the hours spent maintaining a blog.

As recently as a year ago blogs were the darlings of the search engines because search engines "like" new content and relevant keywords, and well-maintained blogs constantly generate new content and relevant keywords. Thus, I believe the primary reason why legal blogs were attracting clients was because search engines "liked" them, not because lawyers' blogging built up any special level of trust that content contained on a firm website could not otherwise engender.

Google recently made changes to its algorithm that diminish the importance of blogging with respect to search engine visibility. Specifically, Google now prioritizes geographic location over content updates and internal keywords in determining which sites are more relevant to a location-specific search query (e.g., "Minneapolis employment lawyer"). Blogging, like anything you do in your practice, should be done the right way or not at all. In order to blog "the right way," solos need to write new posts at least a couple times a week, which can eat up a lot of your precious time. Given my belief that blogging is no longer a highly-effective tool for attracting new business, I recommend that solos use the time they would have spent writing blog entries on updating their firm websites or refining other marketing techniques.

I should note that my advice to eschew blogging only applies to solos whose primary reason for blogging is to market their law practices. Blogging can be fun, therapeutic, and cathartic, and your blog may attract a strong enough following to generate revenue via paid advertisements.

Finally, I concede that guest blogging or commenting on someone else's blog can be a highly effective SEO strategy if the blog allows guest writers to link to their own websites. I also concede that blogging may result in media outlets reaching out to you for a quote if they are doing a story relevant to your practice area because journalists use the "Google machine" just like the rest of us. I imagine, however, that most journalists already have their "go-to guys" when they need a soundbite from a lawyer, and therefore they are unlikely to reach out to you unless you practice in a relatively novel area of law.

VIII. CRAIGSLIST

I put out an ad on Craigslist when I launched my firm because it was free and I had nothing to lose. While the quality of leads Craigslist generated was low, I did locate two clients who found me via Craigslist and the combined fees I earned on those cases was roughly $15,000.

Now that my practice is performing well I believe my time is better spent working on other marketing techniques, but if you are just starting out and do not have many clients, Craigslist is a viable strategy to get your phone ringing.

IX. PAID SEARCH ENGINE ADS

As a preliminary matter, Google's dominance over the search engine market (i.e., over a 70 percent share) is so strong that I do not believe it makes sense for solos with limited marketing budgets to purchase paid ads on any of the other search engines.

As I discussed in a previous section of this chapter, Google generates two types of results when you type a query in the search box: organic (unpaid) and inorganic (paid ads).

Google's most popular paid advertisement product is Pay-Per-Click ("PPC") ads, where advertisers pay Google each time a visitor clicks on their ad. The primary advantage to PPC ads is that your site can get first-page visibility without SEO. I am not a strong proponent of PPC ads because I do not recall a time when I ever clicked on a PPC ad instead of an organic result, and I cannot come up with a good reason why my potential clients would behave differently than me. Accordingly, I view PPC ads mostly as a tool for solos to use as a stopgap while they build their websites' organic visibility.

The main disadvantage to PPC ads is that, depending on the search terms and geography, your PPC campaign can get costly since Google can charge up to $65 per click. I admit this fact tends to contravene my belief that prospective clients do not click on PPC ads, but there is no method to track the percentage of people who click on your PPC ads who then actually pick up the phone to call you.

I concede that paid ads can build trust in your website when coupled with a strong organic listing because the more places your website appears on page one of Google, the more authoritative you seem in the eyes of prospective clients. Given my belief that paid ads are best deployed as a compliment to organic listings, I suggest solos consider two Google products directly tied to their organic listings, Google Tags and Google Boost.

Google Tags (visit www.google.com/help/tags) are the yellow markers that make your organic listing stand out from other listings and allow businesses to highlight certain aspects of their businesses:

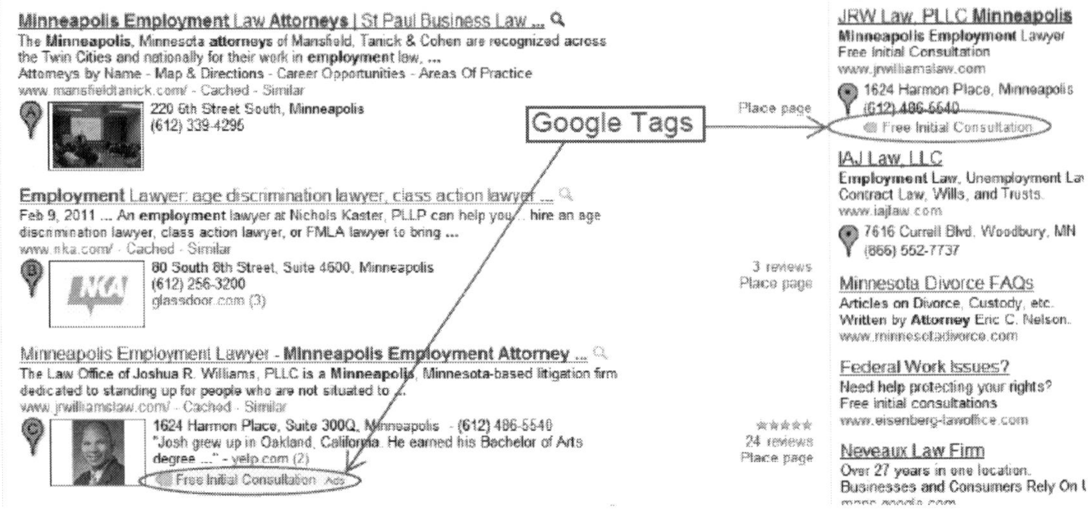

Google Tags costs $25 per month.

Google Boost (visit http://tinyurl.com/64wy2y6) is basically glorified PPC advertising that places a blue bubble next to your ad, but I thought I would try out the product because I like that it is tied to your organic listing, you can set your own monthly budget (minimum $50), and Google will automatically determine what search terms trigger your ad based on your organic listing:

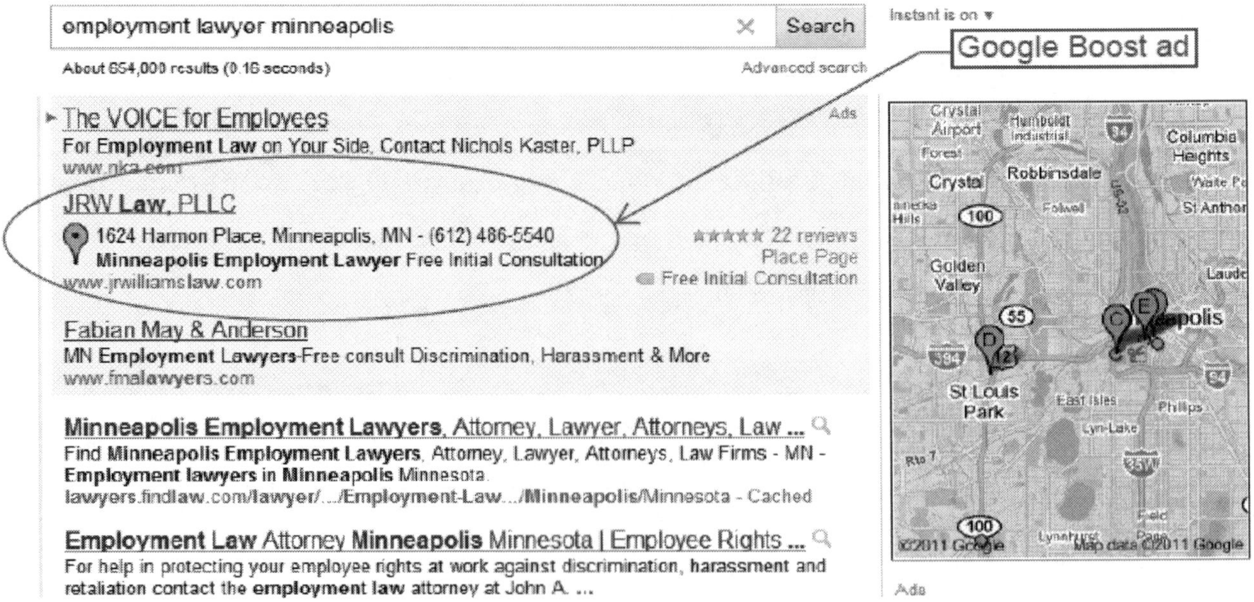

Users must create a free account on Google Places at places.google.com/business in order to use Tags and Boost.

X. SOCIAL MEDIA

While I believe the rise of social media represents a paradigm shift in how people disseminate and consume information, I do not believe building a robust social media presence is a useful strategy for solos to market their practices.

Facebook is a highly visited website, so I suggest solos create profiles that point to their firms' websites because doing so will increase the relevance of their firm sites in the eyes of search engines. Creating a Facebook Place Page (visit http://tinyurl.com/48s6wkz for information on creating a Place Page) may also help your firm's Google ranking. Other than building links to solos' websites, I do not see how Facebook will directly generate clients because I do not know anyone who uses Facebook to look for service providers; people use Facebook to check in on old high school buddies, not to locate attorneys. Your Facebook network could potentially generate a referral or two, but that's about it.

LinkedIn is also a highly visited website, so I suggest solos create profiles for the same reasons they should create Facebook profiles. LinkedIn may also be a good resource for solos to locate established attorneys who can provide mentorship or contract work, and your LinkedIn network may generate a referral or two, but I doubt it is going to generate many clients.

As for Twitter, solos should refrain from publishing tweets in connection with their practices unless they hope to attract the likes of Kim Kardashian and her ilk as clients.

To paraphrase the Zuckerberg character from *The Social Network*, social media is "cool." I may modify my evaluation as social media moves from childhood into pre-adolescence, but at this point, I am unconvinced it is an important marketing tool for solos.

LAWYER 2.0 Other Considerations

I. INTRODUCTION

The scope of this chapter includes consideration of issues that do not fall neatly under previous chapters but still fall under the (broad) aegis of "technology for solos."

II. COMPETENCE

I stated in Chapter 5 that, for solos, good lawyering is a secondary consideration to good marketing. This is not to say I believe that good lawyering is not critically important for solos, as everything I have discussed in this book is aimed at helping solos become more self-reliant, efficient, and organized (i.e., better lawyers). In addition to marketing and management, lawyers must also become proficient in their chosen substantive areas of practice.

If you are a recent law grad or are planning on practicing in an area of law new to you, I highly recommend that you enroll in a CLE course in the area(s) of law you are looking to practice in (if you are a litigator, I also recommend you enroll in courses on motion practice, evidence, depositions, etc.). If you go into a case "blind," it may prejudice your client and expose you to disciplinary action or a malpractice suit. CLEs will also save you time and (in the long run) money because the information you receive at CLEs negates the need to perform the research you would otherwise need to conduct to get up to speed on an area of law. State and local bar associations offer reasonably-priced CLE courses, and if you tell them that you are just starting out and cannot afford the full tuition they may give you a discounted rate or put you on a payment plan.

There are also several services that offer online CLEs. One such service, Solo Practice University (www.solopracticeuniversity.com), is aimed squarely at solos. At $125 per month for unlimited access to dozens of online, prerecorded courses, Solo Practice University seems like a pretty good deal, but I have not utilized the service because I have found that I do not get anything out of CLEs unless I physically attend.

III. OFFICE LOCATION

This section is aimed at solos who are just starting out and deciding where to office.

If you implement the strategies I set forth in this book, you will create a paperless, mobile office that does not require physical space for bulky equipment or storage. Thus, the main considerations when determining where to office are practice area and personal preference.

If your solo practice is still in its embryonic stages I advise you to refrain from locking into a long-term, high-rent lease in a brick-and-mortar location because you may discover that you are not well-suited for solo practice. Accordingly, the most viable options are a true home office; a "virtual office;" a brick-and-mortar office with inexpensive rent or month-to-month leasing; shared office space; or a shared office arrangement with an established firm.

A. True Home Office

If the nature of your practice does not require you to physically meet with clients, or if clients' expectations are that you will come to their location for meetings, a true home office is a good option.

Even if you are someone who has problems getting things done at home and need a dedicated space for work projects, a true home office is still a viable option because you can always go to a coffee shop or the library to work on projects. If you run a high-volume practice where you are constantly taking phone calls, however, working at the library or a coffee shop is not a good option.

If your practice requires you to meet with clients and the expectation is that the client will meet with you at your office, a true home office may not be a good option because you may come across as "small-time" to the client, and it is healthy to establish some boundaries between your work life and non-work life.

I advise solos to refrain from meeting clients at neutral locations such as coffee shops because doing so may defeat the attorney-client privilege and run afoul of the provisions governing client confidentiality contained in the Rules of Conduct. That said, I am acutely sensitive to client confidentiality issues because I have the loudest voice this side of Samuel L. Jackson, so meeting a client at your local Starbucks might not be unreasonable if you know how to modulate your voice.

B. Virtual Office

Virtual offices are ideal for solos whose practice areas require them to meet with clients on a semi-regular basis. Virtual office packages typically include use of meeting and conference rooms on a la carte basis up to a certain number of hours per month, an address at a prime location with a mail forwarding service, a shared receptionist to greet clients, and other administrative services. Virtual office packages typically cost between $100 and $300 per month.

A virtual office may not be a good option if you meet with clients frequently because the cost of renting meeting rooms can get expensive if you exceed your monthly quota of time. Additionally, the mail-forwarding service can create lag-time issues.

C. Brick-and-Mortar Office Space

I chose to rent space in an office building that offered inexpensive, month-to-month leases when I launched my firm because I do not work efficiently from home and I knew my practice—if successful—would require me to meet with clients frequently at a location I provided.

My office arrangement turned out to be less than ideal because the building was a little run-down and located in a somewhat dodgy area, which created image problems for me and perceived safety issues for my clients. Another issue was that the office's lack of a formal waiting area and someone to greet my clients caused daily logistical nightmares. Specifically, my office arrangement precluded me from scheduling back-to-back meetings because if the first appointment arrived late or the second appointment arrived early, the second client would often walk right into my office unannounced in the middle of my first appointment. Such scheduling conflicts required me to awkwardly greet the client and hustle him to the shared conference room (or the chairs outside my hallway if the conference room was occupied) to wait while I concluded my first appointment.

Even after I stopped scheduling back-to-back appointments, my first office arrangement still posed logistical problems. I needed to clear my workspace twenty minutes before an appointment arrived because I did not want prospective clients to see an untidy office if they arrived early, but this often required me to prematurely shut down projects I was working on (e.g., sorting hard copies of documents prior to scanning them in). If a client arrived late or no-showed, then I effectively lost up to an hour of work time.

For the reasons set forth above, I do not recommend a brick-and-mortar office for solos with high-volume practices if it lacks a formal waiting area and someone to greet your appointments.

D. Shared Office Space

Once my practice started taking off, I moved to my current office, which is located in a gorgeous, retrofitted building right across from a park (my office overlooks a pond) in a safe neighborhood just outside Downtown Minneapolis. In addition to negating my safety and image concerns, I am quite satisfied with my current office arrangement because it offers the services of a receptionist shared by the other dozen or so tenants who rent individual offices. The building also has a formal waiting area, two formal conference rooms, and a full, modern kitchen.

E. Shared Office Arrangement with an Established Firm

I think a shared office arrangement at an established firm is ideal for solos just starting out. First, I believe rent is likely to be inexpensive if a firm has an unoccupied office because the firm's owner(s) will probably be grateful to find a tenant and reduce overhead costs. Secondly, if the established firm's areas of practice synergize with your areas of practice you will probably get referrals from the established firm or even some contract work. Third, you can negotiate access to the established firm's resources that may otherwise be outside your budget, including furniture, conference rooms, receptionist, waiting area, phone lines, internet access, etc. Finally, the established firm's owner(s) can provide you with in-house mentorship. As much as I love my office arrangement, I will consider looking for a shared office arrangement when my lease runs out because I sometimes feel isolated being all by myself.

IV. HIRING STAFF

If you implement the strategies set forth in this book, you will be able to run a completely self-sufficient solo practice that negates the need to hire full-time staff (my one caveat to this statement is that if you run a high-volume practice you will need to make sure someone is there to greet your clients, but you can accomplish this through shared office arrangements).

My "support staff" includes a law clerk and a web developer I use on an a la carte basis, and my building has a shared receptionist who greets my clients and lets me know when they arrive. Collectively, my "support staff" averages less than three hours of work per week for me. I should note, however, that the work my "staff" performs is crucial to the success of my practice, but I do not believe you will need full-time staff to build a six-figure practice.

Finally, the nature of my contingency fee practice is such that accounting is fairly simple and I can therefore do my own taxes via online software, but if your billing scheme is more complex you should consider hiring an accountant who specializes in working with solos or small businesses.

V. STARTUP COSTS

Solos can implement every strategy I discussed in this book, including monthly and yearly service fees and first month's rent, for under $6,000, as set forth below (non-essential items in italics):

Hardware	
Laptop	$1,000
Netbook	*$250*
Scanner	$400
Printer	$250
LabelWriter 450	$200
Digital Scale	$30
Seagate Replica	$150
Chill Hub	$40
Wireless Router	$45

Notary Stamp	$150
Web Camera	*$100*
Microphone	*$75*
Deposition DVD	*$130*
DVD Player	*$50*
Tablet PC	*$500*
Wireless Mouse	*$15*
Total	**$3,385**

<u>**Practice Management**</u>

Google Apps for Business	$50/year
Pointofmail.com	$30/year
Virtual Receptionist	$100/month
Cordless Phone System	$75
Phone/Internet Connectivity	$80/month
Smartphone	$100
Wireless Service	$100/month
Documents to Go	$15
Case Management SaaS	$40/month
Internet Fax Service	$10/month
Logo	*$200*
Carbonite	$55/year
Dropbox	Free
Total	**$855**

<u>Paperless Office</u>

Acrobat Pro	$200
Microsoft Office	$150
Shred Service	$25/month
Total	**$375**

<u>Legal Research</u>

Lexis Advance	$175/month
Total	**$175**

<u>Online Marketing</u>

Website	$800
Domain Name	$10/year
Web hosting	$10/month
Google Tags	$25/month
Google Boost	*$50/month*
Total	**$895**

<u>Rent</u>

Virtual Office/Shared Office Arrangement	$300/month
Total	**$300**

GRAND TOTAL ***$5,985***

Subtracting the cost of non-essential items brings your initial startup costs down to about $4,600.

If you are planning on starting a contingency fee firm, I suggest you try to save at least six months' living expenses (factoring in firm overhead, student loans, etc.) prior to launching your solo practice because your cases will take time to reach settlement or verdict. During the period when your cases are percolating through discovery and motion practice, you can look for contract work to generate income.

If you are planning on charging hourly or flat fees, then you can launch your firm without as substantial a nest egg.

If you do not have the luxury of saving up a nest egg prior to launching your firm, you can do what I did and max out your credit cards, slap second mortgages on your house and vehicles to secure loans, and position your nose firmly to the grindstone and hustle hard because failure is not an option.

VI. FINAL THOUGHTS

Launching and running a solo practice can be scary; I have been running my firm for over a year and a half, earned well over $150,000, have thousands in the bank and over 30 clients and I still get scared when I stop to reflect and realize that I need to bring my A-game every day in order to put food on the table for me and my family. What truly terrified me, however, was getting trapped in a job I disliked and living out a mediocre (albeit creature comfortable) existence.

Running my own firm has been the hardest job I have ever had, but it has also been the most rewarding. I hope you are able to implement the strategies set forth in this book to help you build your own rewarding, sustainable solo practice.

-JRW, February 2011

Made in the USA
Monee, IL
05 November 2026

67811375R00081